Cross-Country Running

Jeff Galloway

CROSS-COUNTRY RUNNING

Third Edition

THE BEST TRAINING PLANS FOR PEAK PERFORMANCE IN THE 5K, 1500M, 2000M, AND 10K

Meyer & Meyer Sport

British Library Cataloguing in Publication Data
A catalogue record for this book is available from the British Library

Cross-Country Running
Maidenhead: Meyer & Meyer Sport (UK) Ltd., 2023
ISBN: 978-1-78255-259-8

© 2011, 2012, 2023 by Meyer & Meyer Sport (UK) Ltd.
First edition 2011. Third edition 2023.

Aachen, Auckland, Beirut, Cairo, Cape Town, Dubai, Hägendorf, Hong Kong, Indianapolis, Maidenhead, Manila, New Delhi, Singapore, Sydney, Tehran, Vienna

Member of the World Sport Publishers' Association (WSPA)

Printed by Versa Press, East Peoria, IL
Printed in the United States of America
ISBN: 978-1-78255-259-8

Email: info@m-m-sports.com
www.thesportspublisher.com

Credits
Cover and interior design: Anja Elsen
Layout: Anja Elsen
Cover and interior photos: © AdobeStock
Managing editor: Elizabeth Evans

CONTENTS

DEDICATION

Several years ago, the admissions director of an Ivy League university was asked for one or two high school activities that would give an applicant an advantage in being accepted to his institution, if they were on the waiting list. Without hesitating, he put cross-country at the top of the list. Cross-country runners, he said, have a special type of discipline and are willing to work very hard physically and mentally without receiving recognition. This combination of characteristics produced successful graduates who could handle the pressure-packed university culture.

This book is dedicated to the thousands of cross-country athletes who would not usually be selected for sports that are supported by cheerleaders. On many days, they are huffing, puffing and sweating before most of their fellow students are awake, and have finished a challenging workout before the football players report for practice. They run alone through rain, cold or snow because the workout was listed on the schedule. Exhausted, with half a mile left in a race, they give it everything they have left to help their team.

Cross-country runners sacrifice social activities to study and run. In the process, hidden sources of strength, creativity and confidence are discovered which are applied to everything else in their lives. I dedicate this book to all of those who have discovered the real power of cross-country, and those who are about to do so.

INTRODUCTION

CROSS-COUNTRY CHANGED MY LIFE

Like many children in Navy families, I attended 13 schools by the time I finished the 7th grade. At this point my father became a teacher, we moved to Atlanta, and my new school required each boy to work out with an athletic team after school every day. Because of the moves, I had avoided sports and exercise, did not have sports skills, had become lazy and had gained a lot of weight.

My patchwork of educational experiences had not prepared me for the demanding and competitive academic environment at this prep school, and I was struggling. The principal's comment on the report card was "A little more of a push next year and Jeff will make the top half of the class." I was already studying more hours every week than most of the students I knew, who were scoring better on tests. I believed that I was intellectually inferior.

During the Fall I tried football, which was a total disaster from my perspective, and that of my coaches. Before choosing a sport for the next quarter, I asked several of the other lazy kids for their choices and was surprised to hear that many had chosen Winter Track

Conditioning. The consensus among the slackers was that the track coach was the most lenient in the school. "Tell him you are running on the trails, and you only have to jog 200 yards to the woods and hide out."

I did just that for two days. On the third day, an older athlete I liked looked at me and said "Galloway, you're running with us today." I quickly came up with my strategy: as we entered the woods I planned to grab my hamstring, claiming a muscle pull. But the jokes started right away, and I kept going to hear the punch line. As I began to get really tired, they started telling gossip about the teachers. I didn't last long the first day, but pushed a bit farther with them day after day and started joining the political and psychological arguments.

Most of these cross-country runners were on the academic honor roll. But the controversial arguments led me to believe that I was just as intelligent as the others. Each academic period my grades improved and I, too, made the honor roll. More important, I had become a member of the group and set a new standard for myself due to group expectations.

I was most surprised about how good I felt after a run. The after-run attitude boost was better than I had experienced after any activity during my young life. The camaraderie and fun during those runs kept me coming back and after 10 weeks I was hooked on endorphins and friendship. I continue to be... more than 60 years later.

It was commonly known, even back in the 50s, that over half of the cross-country team members were among the best students and leaders in school organizations. University of Illinois Professor Charles Hillman, as reported by Newsweek magazine, noticed that the women's cross-country team set the curve on his neuroscience/ kinesiology tests every semester. So he started a study of elementary children comparing physical activity with academic achievement. He discovered that the kids who were fitter were also the best students. Various studies around the world have found the following:

- Regular exercise increases the level of BDNF (brain-derived neurotrophic factor), which is necessary for learning, memory and higher brain activities.

- Regular aerobic exercise stimulates growth of new brain cells, at any age.

- Regular vigorous exercise causes existing nerve cells to work quicker and more efficiently.

- Even one 30-minute aerobic exercise session stimulates areas in the brain needed for critical thinking and produces better test results than before the exercise.

So there's more to it than the physical benefits. That experience continues to enrich my life.

A NOTE TO COACHES

Cross-country kids are special. They tend to develop a spirit that drives them in everything they do. As you lead them, you have a chance to help them improve the quality of their lives, for the rest of their lives. The greatest hope is that they will become life long exercisers. Kids who run regularly tend to do better in school and in life.

The process of becoming an athlete adds another wonderful opportunity. Even the kids who join the team to hang out with their friends often surprise themselves and their coaches with their accomplishments. From the first year, most of these first timers have to push themselves to unknown limits. Drawing on the combination of body, mind and spirit they discover that they have more resources than they ever imagined.

With the right combination of nurturing and challenging you can help them learn from each setback and become a significant influence in their lives.

Many of the workouts will be tough. Your challenge is to insert some fun into every day possible. Better yet, set up the dynamics of personalities so that the athletes create the fun. It is possible to have both.

If you enjoy the journey, your athletes will find a way to do so as well.

CHAPTER 1

STAYING INJURY-FREE

The most common reason why cross-country runners don't achieve their goal is that they get injured.

HOW TO STAY INJURY-FREE

1. Be sensitive to your "weak links."

2. Gradually increase the amount of distance.

3. For at least the first two weeks of the preseason, run every other day.

4. Don't do any faster speedwork running during the first three weeks.

5. Fast training needs to be gradually integrated into the schedule.

6. At the first sign of a weak link irritation, reduce training and take 1-2 days off.

7. If there is any question about the severity of the injury, see a doctor who wants you to run.

8. As one returns to running, "stay below the threshold of irritation."

9. Read chapter 19, Injury Prevention and Care, for further details.

CURB THE ENTHUSIASM

During the preseason conditioning and during the first two weeks of cross-country training, most athletes are highly motivated and want to improve quickly. The most common cause of cross-country injuries, in my experience, has been running too fast during this adjustment period, or adding mileage too quickly. In a team setting, early in the season, it's very common to hear runners say, "I should be able to run as fast as John/ Jill," and try to do so. The less conditioned runner can easily get injured during one run by trying to keep up with a teammate who did more training over the summer.

WHY DO WE GET INJURED?

Pushing too hard, too soon, is the most common cause of cross-country injuries that have been reported to me over the decades. Almost all of these can be prevented if runners will begin their training at their current level of conditioning (and not that of a more fit or able friend), gradually increase the duration and intensity, and insert sufficient rest between stress workouts.

Our bodies are programmed to adapt to running by making constant "upgrades" to withstand stress and perform more efficiently. Regular and small increases in workload, followed by recovery periods, promote rebuilding, mechanical and physiological adaptations, and improved capacity. The crucial factor that is most commonly neglected is rest; it is during the recovery period that the rebuilding takes place.

BE SENSITIVE TO YOUR "WEAK LINKS"

These body parts take on more stress when we work out. They are the first to ache, hurt or malfunction when we run a bit too fast or too far—or run too many days in a row. At the first sign of an irritation of a "weak link," take an extra day off as an insurance policy.

MINOR BREAKDOWN SIMULATES IMPROVEMENT

The process starts during a normal workout when micro-tears develop in muscles and tendons due to the focused stress of continued movement/irritation of these key parts. The number of these tiny injuries will increase on long or faster workouts, especially during the last 25%. But in most cases, the rest period after a workout will allow for healing of enough of the damage so that training can continue.

Stopping a workout when an injury occurs, and taking 2-3 days off at the beginning of an injury, can promote almost complete healing, or get the healing started. The first day back should be gentle and short. If there are no signs of injury, training can continue without compromising race performance at the end of the season. But running even the last mile of a workout with an injury can increase the damage dramatically and may limit the training for the rest of the season.

COMMON WEAK LINKS:

Joints—knee, hip, ankle
Muscles—calf, hamstring, quadriceps
Tendons—Achilles tendon, knee, ankle
Soft tissue (Fascia)—especially around joints, foot
Bones—foot and leg
Nerve tissue—foot and leg
Feet and ankle—just about any area can be overstressed in cross-country

MOST INJURIES ARE NOT FELT DURING THE WORKOUT THAT PRODUCES THEM

In some cases, pain-killing hormones, such as endorphins, will mask the damage at first. Even when the first aches and pains occur, most runners go into denial, ignore the first symptoms, and train until the stressed area breaks down. This usually results in significant downtime for repair or a significant reduction in performance for the season, or both.

HOW TO SUSTAIN PROGRESS AND AVOID INJURY

- A slight increase in training duration or intensity produces a minor breakdown of tissue. This stimulates each area that has been abused to adapt to a higher workload.

- If the rest between the challenging workouts is sufficient for the individual, the muscles, tendons, joints, feet, etc. rebuild stronger to accommodate a projected higher workload in the near future. For beginners this rest period is often 48 hours in the preseason and the early stages of the season. Veteran runners can often run easily, every other day, and avoid breakdown—but some veterans need at least 2 days off from running per week, strategically placed.

- During the days off, cross-training can provide other benefits, while the body is improving. Deep water running, for example can improve running efficiency. All body parts continue to adapt in structure, efficiency, and performance when there is a balance between workout stress and rest.

RUNNING IMPROVEMENT CONTINUES IF...

- We don't push too far beyond current capabilities.
- We engage in regular workouts.
- One or two workouts a week push the intensity or duration a bit further than before.
- Sufficient rest is provided after the stressful sessions as rebuilding time.

CHAPTER 2

THE INSIDE STORY ON GETTING FASTER

By running easily and regularly, the whole body works together to help you move more efficiently while you increase your positive health potential. Lungs become more efficient; the heart is strengthened. Oxygen is processed more efficiently into the blood, and the blood is pumped more effectively through the body. At the same time, your leg muscles, tendons, joints, etc., make up a strong and coordinated system to gradually do more work, and move you farther and faster down the road.

When you decide to test yourself through speed training and racing, you take certain risks to prepare for a number of rewards. Speed training is necessary for maximum time improvement, but it will dramatically increase the risk of injury. The quest toward a time goal can send the ego on a trip that reduces running enjoyment due to the narrow focus on a time goal.

The regular but gentle increase of speed repetitions stimulates the body to improve the efficiency of the mechanical workings of the feet, legs, and joints. Behind the scenes, the mitochondria (inner powerhouses that process energy) are pushed into delivering more, even when under duress. Individual muscle cells act as pumps, helping to return blood to the heart and lungs. By testing yourself in speed sessions and races, you will be challenging your "physiological team" to achieve a higher level of performance.

GETTING FASTER REQUIRES EXTRA WORK

To get faster, we must push beyond our current, comfortable levels. All of us have a lazy streak in us. Our bodies are programmed to conserve resources by doing the smallest amount of work they can get away with. So even after we have increased the length of our runs, steadily over several months, our leg muscles, tendons, and liagments are not prepared for the jolt that speed training delivers. But only when we put the legs, the heart, and the lungs to a gentle test, week by week, does the body respond by improving in dozens of ways. The best way to stay injury free is to gradually increase the duration and intensity, eliminating the "jolt."

TEAMWORK

When stressed, the heart, lungs, muscles, tendons, central nervous system, brain, blood system are programmed to work as a team. The right brain intuitively solves problems, manages resources, and fine-tunes various processes mentioned above so that you can run faster.

THE LONG RUN BUILDS ENDURANCE AND A BETTER PLUMBING SYSTEM

By gradually extending slow long runs, you train muscle cells to expand their capacity to utilize oxygen efficiently, sustain energy production, and in general, increase capacity to go farther. Continually increasing distance during long runs increases the reach of blood artery capillaries to deliver oxygen, and promote the return of waste products so that the muscles can work at top capacity. In short, long runs bestow a better plumbing system, resulting in a greater muscle workload. These changes will pay off when you do speed training.

ENDORPHINS KILL PAIN AND MAKE YOU FEEL GOOD

When you run, at any pace, your body intuitively knows there will be some pain. This stimulates the production of natural painkillers called endorphins. These hormones act as drugs that can both relax and invigorate you with vitality, while bestowing a good attitude—even when tired after the run. If the rest interval is just right, you'll feel them kicking in between faster segments of speed workouts.

GRADUALLY PUSHING UP THE WORKLOAD

Your body is programmed to improve when it is gradually introduced to a little more work, with enough rest afterward. Push too hard, or neglect the rest, and you'll see an increase in aches, pains, and injury. By balancing the speed workouts, adjusting for problems, and having realistic goals, most runners can continue to improve throughout the season.

STRESS + REST = IMPROVEMENT

When we run a little faster than our realistic goal pace, and increase the workload a little more than we did on last week's speed workout, this tends to slightly break down the muscle cells, tendons, etc. just enough to stimulate change. You see, our bodies are programmed to rebuild stronger than before, but there must be gentle and regular stress, followed by significant rest.

INTRODUCING THE BODY TO SPEED THROUGH TWO WEEKS OF "DRILLS"

As a gentle introduction to faster running, I've found nothing better than the two drills that are detailed in chapter 14: Turnover Drills and Acceleration-Gliders. The former helps to improve cadence of the legs and feet. The latter provides a very gentle introduction to speedwork, in very short segments. Most of the running during the conditioning period is at an easy pace. These drills, done in the middle of a run, once or twice a week, will improve mechanics, get the muscles ready for the heavier demands of speed training, and initiate internal physiological changes in the muscles—with very little risk of injury. DON'T COMPETE WITH OTHER RUNNERS DURING THESE DRILLS.

A GENTLE INCREASE IN YOUR WEEKLY WORKOUTS CAUSES A SLIGHT BREAKDOWN

The weekly speed workout starts with a few speed repetitions, with rest between each. As the number of repetitions increase each week, your body is pushed slightly beyond what it did the previous week. In each workout, your muscle fibers get tired as they reach the previous maximum workload, and continue to keep you running the pace assigned. In every session some are pushed beyond their capacity with each additional repetition. Often, the pain and fatigue are not felt during the workout. But within one or two days there are usually sore muscles and tendons, and general overall tiredness. Even walking may not feel smooth for a day or two after a really hard speed session.

THE DAMAGE

Looking inside the cell at the end of a hard workout, you'll see damage:

- Tears in the muscle cell membrane.

- The mitochondria (energy processors inside the cell) are swollen.

- There's a significant lowering of the muscle stores of glycogen (the energy supply needed in speedwork).

- Waste products from exertion, bits of bone and muscle tissue and other bio junk can be found.

- Sometimes, there are small tears in the blood vessels and arteries, and blood leaks into the muscles.

THE MUSCLES REBOUND, STRONGER AND BETTER THAN BEFORE

Gentle overuse stimulates your body to not only repair the damage, but rebuild it stronger. The process puts the body on alert to be ready for more hard work, and to repair damage better next time.

Two days after a speed session, if the muscles have had enough rest, you'll see some improvements:

- Waste has been removed.

- Thicker cell membranes can handle more work without breaking down.

- The mitochondria have increased in size and number, so that they can process more energy next time.

- The damage to the blood system has been repaired.

- Over several months, after adapting to a continued series of small increases, more capillaries (tiny fingers of the blood system) are produced, improving and expanding the delivery of oxygen and nutrients and providing a better withdrawal of waste products.

These are only some of the many adaptations made by the incredible human body when we exercise: biomechanics, nervous system, strength, muscle efficiency and more. Internal psychological improvements follow the physical ones. Mind, body and spirit are becoming part of the process of improving health and performance. An added benefit is a positive attitude.

QUALITY REST IS CRUCIAL: 48 HOURS BETWEEN WORKOUTS

Without sufficient rest, the damage won't be totally repaired. On rest days, it's important to avoid exercises that strenuously use the calf muscle, ankle and Achilles tendon (stair machines, step aerobics, spinning out of the saddle) for the 48-hour period between running workouts. If you have other aches and pains from your individual "weak links," then don't do exercises that aggravate them further. Walking is usually a great exercise for a rest day. There are several other good exercises in chapter 17, Cross-Training. As long as you are not continuing to stress the calf, most alternative exercises are fine.

BEWARE OF JUNK MILES

A high percentage of injuries are caused by running more than is recommended on the schedule. If the "easy days" are not easy enough, the weak links cannot rebuild. The short, "junk mile" days don't help your conditioning, and they interfere with recovery.

REGULARITY

To maintain the adaptations, you must regularly run about every 2 days. To maintain the speed improvements mentioned in this book, you'll need to do at least one speed workout per week, every week. Cadence drills and acceleration-gliders will continue to improve running efficiency if each drill is done at least once a week.

"MUSCLE MEMORY"

Your neuromuscular system remembers the patterns of muscle activity which you have done regularly over an extended period of time. The longer you have been running regularly, the more easily it will be to start up when you've had a layoff. During your first few months of speedwork, for example, if you miss a weekly workout, you will need to drop back a week, and rebuild. Be careful as you return to speed training, if this happens.

TIP: CRAMPED FOR TIME? JUST DO A FEW REPETITIONS

Let's say that you cannot get to the track on your speed day, and you don't have but 15 minutes to run. Take a 3-4 minute slow warm-up with some accelerations, and do the same during the last 3-5 minutes. During the middle 5-9 minutes, run several 1-2 minute accelerations at approximately the pace you would run on the track. Don't worry if the pace is not perfect. Any of these segments is better than a week without any fast running at all.

AEROBIC RUNNING IS DONE DURING LONG RUNS

Aerobic means "in the presence of oxygen." This is the type of running you do when you feel "slow" and comfortable—with no huffing and puffing. When running aerobically, your muscles can get enough oxygen from the blood to process the energy in the cells. The minimal waste products produced during aerobic running can be easily removed, with no lingering build-up in the muscles.

SPEED TRAINING GETS YOU INTO THE ANAEROBIC ZONE

Anaerobic running means running too fast or too long for you, on that day. At some point in the workout, when you reach your current limit, the muscles can't get enough oxygen to burn the most efficient fuel, fat. So they shift to the limited supply of stored carbohydrate: glycogen. The waste products from this fuel pile up quickly in the cells, tightening the muscles and causing you to breathe heavily. This is called an oxygen debt. If you keep running for too long in this anaerobic state, you will have to slow down significantly or stop. But if you are running for a realistic time goal, and are pacing yourself correctly, you should only be running anaerobically for a short period of time, at the end of each speed workout.

THE ANAEROBIC THRESHOLD

As you increase the quantity of your speed sessions, you'll push back the anaerobic threshold. This means that you can run a bit farther than before—each week, at the same pace, without extreme huffing and puffing. Your muscles can move your body farther and faster without going to exhaustion. Each speed workout pushes you a little bit more into the anaerobic zone. Speed improvement requires running with an oxygen debt. Speed training teaches the body and mind that they can go farther before going anaerobic, how to deal with the discomfort of this, and how to keep going when the muscles are tight and tired. It also tells you that you don't have to give up on performance when in this state.

HOW AEROBIC ARE YOU? THE TALK TEST

You're aerobic—if you can talk for as long as you want with minimal huffing & puffing (h & p)

You are mostly aerobic—if you can talk for 30 sec + then must h & p for 5-10 seconds

You are approaching the anaerobic threshold—if you can only talk for 10 seconds or less, then h & p for 10+ sec

You're anaerobic—if you can't talk more than a few words, and are mostly huffing and puffing

FAST TWITCH VS. SLOW TWITCH MUSCLE FIBERS

We are born with a combination of two types of muscle fibers. Those with a high percentage of fast twitchers can run fast for a short distance, and then become very tired. Fast twitch fibers are designed to burn glycogen (stored carbohydrate) in your muscles. This is the fuel we use during the first 15 minutes of exercise, and it can produce a lot of waste product, such as lactic acid. If we run even a little too fast at the beginning of a run, the muscles will become very tight and tired, very quickly. You will huff and puff, and feel increasingly uncomfortable.

If you have a higher percentage of slow twitch fibers, you won't be able to run as fast at first, but can keep going for longer distances. Slow twitch fibers burn more fat—a fuel that is very efficient and produces little waste product. Long runs will not only condition the slow twitch fibers to work to top capacity as they efficiently burn fat, but as you increase the length of the long ones, you'll train some of your fast twitch fibers to burn fat as fuel.

Once the starting pace is controlled (and also the ego), fast runners develop a mix of fast and slow twitchers to do the work of running, and find that they don't get exhausted at the end. On long runs it is crucial to stay aerobic by running very slowly, and inserting walk breaks. This allows one to push back the endurance limit, while recovering fast.

MENTAL CHANGES—BOTH POSITIVE AND NEGATIVE

When runners get more fit, their mental attitude changes in many positive ways. While self-confidence improves, a more positive attitude emerges. You'll deal better with stress, improve general outlook on life, and have mental momentum for the stress of competition and other challenges in life.

ARE YOU WORKING TOO HARD ON A TIME GOAL?

When runners get too focused on specific time goals they often find more stress and some negative attitude changes. At the first sign of these symptoms, back off and let mind and body get back together again:

- Running is not as enjoyable.
- You don't look forward to your runs.
- When you say something to others about your running, the statements are often negative.
- The negativity can permeate into other areas of your life.
- You look on running as work instead of play.

THE PERSONAL GROWTH OF SPEED TRAINING

Instead of looking just at the times in your races, embrace the life lessons that can come from the journey of an extended speed training program. Most of your runs must have some fun in them, to help you through this journey. Even after a hard workout, focus on how good you feel afterward, and the satisfaction from meeting the challenge.

The reality of a speed training program is that you'll have more setbacks than victories. But you will learn more from the setbacks and they will make you a smarter runner, and a stronger person. Confronting challenges is initially tough, but leads you to some of the great treasure of the improvement process. As you dig for deeper resources you find that you have more strength inside than you thought.

NOTE: There's more on this topic in chapter 27, Mental Toughness.

CHAPTER 3

SMART SPEEDWORK = FASTER RACES

World class runners have known for decades that training for a shorter race will get the racng systems ready to run faster in the longer event. The same principle applies to cross-country racing. The faster pace of both the workouts and the race itself forces the muscles, tendons, nerves, cardiovascular system, psyche, and spirit to "gear up." But if athletes run too fast for their current conditioning, injuries and exhaustion limit performance.

The regularity of the workouts sets up a process of improving efficiency, as well as a system of searching for the resources needed to encounter challenges not faced before. For example, once you have trained to run faster, at the half-mile distance, the pace for a one or two mile race seems easier. You also tend to feel smoother when you run this longer distance. That is one reason for the time trials (PTT) listed in chapter 4.

TRAINING AT A PACE THAT IS FASTER THAN RACE PACE CHALLENGES THE SYSTEM TO IMPROVE

Each week, as you add to the work done in your speed workout, you slightly overwhelm the muscles and cardiovascular system. Your body has the incredible capacity to respond to this challenge by rebuilding stronger than before, with better efficiency.

THE FASTER SPEEDWORK PRODUCES SYSTEMS THAT PERFORM AT A HIGHER CAPACITY

The faster pace of your speed workout coaxes adaptations out of the tendons, muscles and nervous system. You touch lighter and use your ankle and leg muscles more efficiently, while building the strength necessary to run faster.

SUSTAINED SPEED—THROUGH AN INCREASE IN THE NUMBER OF REPETITIONS

Sprint speed provides little or no benefit in a cross-country race. Speed repetitions are run about 30 sec/mile faster than goal pace. As you increase the number of speed repetitions from 4 to 6 to 8 and beyond, you teach yourself how to keep going at your assigned pace, even when tired. The only way to prepare for this "race reality" situation is to do this during speed training. Speedwork prepares you to keep going when the legs usually would slow down.

LONGER RUNS MAINTAIN ENDURANCE AND IMPROVE YOUR TIME

Your long runs will maintain or extend endurance while you improve speed. Every week or two you'll run a very slow longer run. Long runs improve your cardiovascular infrastructure, so that you can achieve higher capacity through speedwork and in the races.

RUNNING FORM IMPROVES

Regular speed workouts stimulate your body to run more efficiently. During each workout, as you push into fatigue, your body intuitively searches for ways of continuing to move at the same pace without extraneous motion: lighter touch of the feet, direct foot lift, lower to the ground, quicker turnover.

WATCH OUT! SPEEDWORK INCREASES ACHES, PAINS AND INJURIES

Speed training increases your chance of injury. Be sensitive to the areas on your foot, leg, muscles, etc., where you have had problems before. Think back to the patterns of aches and pains that have caused you to reduce or stop exercise in the past. You can reduce the chance of injury significantly by taking a day of two off at the flare-up of one of these, and by following the tips in chapter 19, Injury Prevention and Care.

CHAPTER 4

PREDICTING PERFORMANCE AND MEASURING PROGRESS

The most important part of training for a goal is choosing one that is realistic.

By using a program that is based upon a realistic improvement strategy, you gain a significant amount of control over your training. Through planning and time trials, you'll glimpse into the your racing future, while preparing the mind for the challenge.

- A series of regular time trials tell you what goal is realistic (based upon formulas in this chapter).

- Weekly speed sessions develop the capacity to run faster.

- As you increase the number of repetitions during your training, you stimulate all of the systems to keep going—even when tired.

You'll increase the potential for success greatly with a proven plan, improve your confidence, while you enjoy the satisfaction from being on a journey or mission that means something to you.

SETTING UP YOUR PLAN FOR SUCCESS

1. Set the date or dates for your primary goal (up to a 5% improvement).

2. Pace of speed repetitions is about 30 sec/mile faster than goal pace.

3. Run a series of "prediction time trials" (PTT) to monitor progress, as noted in the schedule.

4. Use the prediction formula to see what you are ready to run at the end of the program.

5. Do a regular series of time trials to monitor your progress.

YOUR GOAL RACE: THE FINAL EXAM

Once you have decided on your primary goal for this year, you've made the most important decision. Write this down in your calendar or journal. This is your "deadline" around which the other races and training elements are scheduled. If you tend to race all-out in every race, you may need to keep reminding yourself throughout your journey that the final exam is the main goal, and your other races serve to evaluate the training as they improve your speed conditioning.

CHOOSE THE DISTANCE OF YOUR PREDICTION TIME TRIAL

Your primary goal race will determine which test races you choose and then which training program you will use in this book. It is best to run these on a track to have a standard for comparison.

Primary mission	The PTT
5K	1 mile
2 mile/3000 meters	1 mile
1500 meters	800 meters
1 mile	800 meters

PREDICTING RACE PERFORMANCE

The formula that I recommend to you is the result of more than four decades of coaching and working with over 250,000 runners.

GUIDELINES FOR USING THE FORMULAS

- You have done the training necessary for the goal—according to the training programs in this book.

- You are not injured.

- You run with an even-paced effort.

- The weather on race day is not adverse.

THE TIME TRIAL RESULT PREDICTS THE IDEAL UNDER PERFECT CONDITIONS

- This is the best time one could currently predict in a track race, at the longer distance.

- Rough terrain, hills, weather, crowds, etc. will result in slower times on cross-country courses.

- By comparing runner's times on a track vs. the same distance on each cross-country course, one can establish a "conversion factor" to predict specific performance on specific courses.

- Experienced coaches can give good estimates based upon these differences.

WORKOUT GROUPING

The times recorded in the time trials allow for runners to be grouped into current workout pace groups of comparable ability.

Long run pace should be at least 3 minutes slower than the per-mile pace of the race pace predicted by the PTT. It's better to run even slower than this, to reduce injury.

THE FIRST PREDICTION TIME TRIAL (PTT)

1. Go to a track, or other accurately measured course.

2. Warm up by walking for 5 minutes, then running easily for 5-10 minutes. New runners should take a 30 second walk break every 1-3 minutes during this warm-up.

3. Do 4 acceleration-gliders. These are listed in chapter 14.

4. Walk for 3-4 minutes.

5. Run the distance of your PTT.

6. On your first time trial, don't run all-out from the start—ease into your pace after the first half of the distance.

7. On each successive time trial, try to run faster than the previous best.

8. Don't sprint!

9. Warm down by reversing the warm-up.

10. If you use a GPS measured segment, use the same segment for each PTT.

11. Use the following table to see how you are doing.

 NOTE: Be sure to convert the PTT Time into minutes and hundredths of a minute. For example, a 6:24 magic mile would be 6.40 minutes

TO PREDICT YOUR TIME IN A 1 MILE:

Test Race is 800 meters (two laps around a track). Simply take your 800 meter time and do the math.

GOAL RACE PREDICTION FORMULA

Mile multiply by 2.22

TO PREDICT YOUR 2 MILE OR 5K PERFORMANCE:

Use the "Magic Mile" (4 laps around the track)

- 2 mile prediction: take your one mile time and multiply by 2.1

- 5K prediction: take your one mile time and multiply by 3.4

THE "LEAP OF FAITH" GOAL PREDICTION

It is OK to choose a time for your goal race which is faster than is predicted by your first PTT. As you do the speed training, the long runs and your test races, you should improve.

As you take this "leap" to a goal, I suggest no more than a 5% improvement in a 2-3 month training program.

GOAL IMPROVEMENT OVER A 2-3 MONTH TRAINING PROGRAM

Pre-test prediction in race time	3% Improvement	5% Improvement
33 minutes	60 seconds	1 minute 40 seconds
28 minutes	50 seconds	1 minute 24 seconds
25 minutes	45 seconds	1 minute 15 seconds
20 minutes	36 seconds	60 seconds
17 minutes	31 seconds	51 seconds
14 minutes	25 seconds	42 seconds
12 minutes	21 seconds	36 seconds

The key to goal setting is keeping your ego in check. From my experience, I have found that a 3% improvement is realistic because cross-country courses produce slower times than the same distance on a track. This means that if your goal race time is predicted to be 20 minutes at the beginning of the season, it is realistic to assume that you could lower it by 36 seconds if you do the speed training and the long runs as noted on my training schedules.

The predictions assume that everything must come together to produce the predicted result. You make the goal prediction come true by doing the speedwork, drills, long runs, etc. that are necessary for your goal. In the speed workouts, you'll run segments that are faster than goal pace. Read chapter 3 and the training program chapters 7-12 to see how this works.

A SERIES OF PTTS

During certain time trial days, as noted on the training schedule, you can record your times and chart your progress.

- Follow the same format as listed in the first predicted PTT.

- By doing this regularly, you will get better at pacing yourself.

- Hint: it's better to start a bit more slowly than you think you can run.

- Walk breaks will be helpful for most beginning runners at a pace that is 10 min/mi or slower. Read chapter 18 on the Run-Walk-Run method for suggestions.

- See how you're doing—do the math after each test.

- If you are not making progress, then look for reasons and adjust training and pacing.

REASONS WHY YOU MAY NOT BE IMPROVING:

1. You're over trained and tired—if so, reduce your training, and/or take an extra rest day.

2. You may have chosen a goal that is too ambitious for your current ability.

3. You may have missed some of your workouts, or not been as regular with your training.

4. The temperature may have been above 65°F (16°C). Heat will slow you down.

5. When using different test courses, one of them may not have been accurately measured.

FINAL REALITY CHECK

The last two time trials are crucial for predicting your race pace. Average the times from these two tests to get a good prediction on a track, and then make the estimated conversion due to terrain, hills, etc. Experienced coaches can often estimate the slowdown on specific courses, based upon experience.

Week of Jan 1

Just getting out there three times a week means you're taking responsibility for your health. When you learn to enjoy those three outings you're taking charge of your attitude.

- Be careful with Achilles tendon.
- Build long one to 18! (must slow down in beginning).
- Slow down in the beginning of each run!

std = standard course; inj = injury; sp = speed; lr = long run; sc = scenic; tr = transcendental; gr = group run; adj = adjustment; fn = fun; fb = fat burning; ntr = nutrition; mt = mental training; ag = afterglow; so = social

Monday — Jan 1

Goal:	35 min easy	1
Run/Walk/Run* strategy used:	w/4-8 form accels	2
Time:	31 min	3
Distance:	@ 3 mi	4
AM Pulse:	52	5
Weather:	rainy - cold	6
Temp:	27°	7
Time:	5 AM(PM)	8
Terrain:	rolling	9
Walk Break:	none	10

Comments:
- Cloudy day - dreary. Had to force myself out.
- Left Achilles felt tender - should have iced it but didn't.
- This is the year to enjoy running!

Tuesday — Jan 2

Goal:	45 min easy	1
Run/Walk/Run* strategy used:	(sn)	2
Time:	52 min	3
Distance:	doesn't matter	4
AM Pulse:	51	5
Weather:	sunny - dry	6
Temp:	48°	7
Time:	6 AM(PM)	8
Terrain:	mixed	9
Walk Break:	-	10

Comments:
- Very (t)
- Sunrise
- One of those rare days when the body didn't want to..but the spirit craved for transcendental excition.
- New trail along river
- Very slow + very peaceful! (went slow in beginning - it worked!)

Wednesday — Jan 3

Goal:	off - XT	1
Run/Walk/Run* strategy used:	run in H₂O	2
Time:	33 min	3
Distance:	-	4
AM Pulse:	52	5
Weather:	-	6
Temp:	-	7
Time:	6 AM(PM)	8
Terrain:	-	9
Walk Break:	-	10

Comments:
- (5 sets of 10) arm running weights H₂O
- 3 sets of 2 minutes then 15 min easy => new floatation belt
- walk for 15 min with Barb

Thursday — Jan 4

Goal:	35 min easy	1
Run/Walk/Run* strategy used:	(sc)	2
Time:	45 min	3
Distance:	@ 6.5	4
AM Pulse:	49	5
Weather:	cloudy	6
Temp:	40°	7
Time:	6 AM PM	8
Terrain:	rolling	9
Walk Break:		10

Comments:
- Great run with Barb, Wes + Sambo - who took out the pace too fast
+ died at the end. The rest of us caught up on the gossip.
- Achilles ached so I iced it for 15 minutes.

Friday — Jan 5

Goal:	45 min (sp)	1
Run/Walk/Run* strategy used:	5 x 800 meter	2
Time:	1:15	3
Distance:	1-5 mi	4
AM Pulse:	53	5
Weather:	sunny	6
Temp:	45°	7
Time:	5 AM(PM)	8
Terrain:	track	9
Walk Break:	400 m	10

Comments:
- 2.30 My best workout in years!
- 2.36
- 2.33 - walked 400 m between each
- 2.37 - struggled on last one
- 2.32
- 2.36 Achilles ached - iced 15 min
- 12 min warm up and warm down

Saturday — Jan 6

Goal:	off	1
Run/Walk/Run* strategy used:		2
Time:	-	3
Distance:	-	4
AM Pulse:	55	5
Weather:	-	6
Temp:	-	7
Time:	- AM PM	8
Terrain:	-	9
Walk Break:	-	10

Comments:
- Kids soccer (mom)
Westin scores goal bouncing off his back 1st goal of season!
- Brennan's cross country (aft) Invitational
Brennan comes from 8th to 3rd in the last half mile. I'm so proud!

Sunday — Jan 7

Goal:	18 mi (l)	1
Run/Walk/Run* strategy used:	easy	2
Time:	2.53	3
Distance:	18 mi	4
AM Pulse:	52	5
Weather:	dry - no wind	6
Temp:	50°	7
Time:	7 AM(PM)	8
Terrain:	flat	9
Walk Break:	1 min/mi	10

Comments:
- It was great to cover 18 miles - wish I had a group
- longest run in 18 months! but...
- went too fast in the first 5 miles
- Achilles hurt afterward - take 3 days off

USE A JOURNAL!

Your chance of reaching your goal increases greatly with this very important instrument, and luckily, you can buy my *Your Personal Running Journal*, which is already set up for you to record your daily run workouts, and includes additional tips for training. Psychologically, you start taking responsibility for the fulfillment of your mission when you use a journal.

CHAPTER 5

PRESEASON CONDITIONING

 NOTE: All of the normal rules apply about getting medical clearance before the athlete begins strenuous exercise. If there are injuries, get medical advice from a doctor. Information in this book is not intended to be medical advice but rather is given only as advice from one runner to another.

SHOES

It's best to go to a running store with the most experienced staff. Spend a little time to get a training shoe that will last the season. Be sure to read the shoe section in this chapter concerning breaking the shoe in, and other issues.

CROSS-TRAINING

During the preseason it's best to run only 3 days a week, with a day off from running between. This allows the body to gently adapt to the running motion. On the off day, overall conditioning will be improved by doing some form of cross-training. The best mode for running is deep water running, with feet off the bottom of the pool. An aquajogger flotation belt is recommended (for more information, see *www.JeffGalloway. com*). This activity can improve running form. On cross- training days, avoid activities that fatigue the calf muscle: stair machines, rowing machines, spinning or leg strengthening exercises.

NO HUFFING AND PUFFING ON PRESEASON RUNS

The best sign that an athlete is reducing injury risk is a reduced breathing rate. If one is breathing heavily at any point, slow down, and take more walk breaks. Rapid breathing at the end of the run means that the pace needs to be reduced, from the beginning, on the next run.

The following is a training program for those who are starting from zero running. Those who have been running for at least two months (three or more times per week) could use the "Veteran Runners" schedule.

ACCELERATION-GLIDERS (ON WEDNESDAY)

This drill is inserted into the middle of your Wednesday run. (Read more in chapter 14.) These simple exercises introduce your muscles to faster running, gradually. Don't count the number of steps—this is only given as a general reference.

1. Jog very slowly for about 15 strides.

2. Jog faster for about 15 strides.

3. Over the next 20 strides, gradually increase pace. Don't come close to a sprint, just run faster than a fast jog. On each successive Acg (acceleration glide) you could run just a little bit faster. Don't increase stride length much—use a quicker turnover of the feet and legs, touching lightly with the feet. Don't compete with other runners during this drill—let yourself gradually warm up.

4. Then glide! The most effective part of the drill is training yourself how to use your momentum to glide or coast gradually down to a jog. At first you will only be able to do a few strides. If you do this once a week, you'll find yourself going farther on each "glide" after several weeks.

5. During the first week, do only two of these. During the second week do no more than 4. From that point, repeat this 4-8 times.

6. To maintain your progress in this activity, do this every week. It is a great way to warm up before PTT, and all of the hill and speed workouts.

 NOTE: Increasing speed will increase injury risk. Reduce this risk significantly by gradually increasing speed, and being sensitive to all "weak link" areas that tend to get sore or painful when you run farther or faster than you have been running. When in doubt, back off the pace, at least in the beginning of the workout, and provide more rest between runs.

TERRAIN TRAINING

It's best to have one or two workouts a week on the same type of terrain you will be racing on. During the preseason conditioning, this could begin after the first week, but only one or two days a week. Gradually introduce the body to uneven terrain by warming up on a stable surface (about 10 minutes), then alternating between 100-200 yards of terrain, followed by 100-200 yards of stable surface running. Start with 4-8 short segments and finish each run with an easy 10-15 minutes on stable terrain.

Those who have problems with unstable terrain need to be careful and should use an even more conservative approach to the terrain than suggested here. All runners should run these terrain segments slowly during the preseason training period.

After the first terrain session, if there are no problems, the same format can be used once or twice a week, gradually increasing the number of segments to 10 for beginners and 20 for advanced. During the third week, the distance of the terrain segments could be increased to 200 yards for beginners and 400 yards for advanced. Once the regular season starts, runners could pick up the pace on some of the segments—but no sprinting. During the last 3 weeks of the season, most runners have adapted to the uneven terrain and can do one quality workout each week that is mostly run on the type of surface used in upcoming races. A warm-up and warm-down on stable terrain is suggested, however.

NEW OR "COMEBACK" RUNNERS:

Preseason conditioning program

(A "comeback" runner has run before but hasn't run for a while.)

XT means "cross-training" (water running for 20-30 minutes is best)

*   means "cadence drill" (4-8) done on Wednesday
**   means acceleration-glider drill, embedded in the run for that day (4-8)

Walk breaks are recommended on all runs—follow the suggestions here, based upon pace per mile

Mon	Tues	Wed*	Thu	Fri	Sat	Sun (5K)	(1mi XC)
Week 1							
Run 10 min	off/XT	Run 13 min	off/XT	Run 16 min	off	1.5 mi	(.5mi)
Week 2							
Run 17 min	off/XT	Run 20 min	off/XT	Run 23 min	off	2.0 mi	(.75)
Week 3**							
Run 23 min	off/XT	Run 26 min	off/XT	Run 30 min	off	2.5 mi	(1 mi)
Week 4**							
Run 30 min	off/XT	Run 30 min	off /XT	Run 30 min	off	3.0 mi	(1.25mi)

WALK BREAKS FOR NEW RUNNERS

Walk breaks will ease the feet and legs into running and can virtually eliminate injuries during the preseason (with conservative pacing). I have heard thousands of reports from beginners who would not have started running without using walk breaks, did not get discouraged because they took walk breaks, or actually ran faster when they compared times with and without taking walk breaks. Many beginners who took liberal walk breaks during their first year learned to like the cross-country experience and improved every year. By the third or fourth year some were the top 5 runners on their teams.

Here is the recommendation for walk breaks based upon pace per mile. An easy way for the various groups to monitor these is to use the run-walk-run interval timer available at *www.JeffGalloway.com*. Remember that by choosing a pace that is much slower than one could run, with liberal walk breaks during the first 2 weeks, the risk of injury is reduced significantly. Once you choose a pace per mile, here are the recommended portions of running and walking.

Pace/mile	Run-Walk-Run strategy
8 min/mile	run 4 minutes/walk 30 seconds
8:30 min/mile	run 3 min/walk 30 seconds
9 min/mile	run 2 min/walk 30 seconds
9:30 min/mile	run 1:45-2 min/walk 30 seconds
10 min/mile	run 90 seconds/walk 30 seconds
10:30 min/mile	run 75 seconds/walk 30 seconds
11 min/mile	run 75-60 seconds/walk 30 seconds
12 min/mile	run 60 seconds/walk 30 seconds
13 min/mile	run 30 seconds/walk 30 seconds or 20/20
14 min/mile	30/30 or 20/20 or 15/15 or run 20/walk 30
15 min/mile	run 15 seconds/walk 30 seconds
16 min/mile	run 10 seconds/walk 30 second

VETERAN RUNNERS:

Pre-season conditioning program

 NOTE: Veterans who have not been running much should follow the lower amount of running listed on each day.

XT means "cross training" (water running for 20-30 minutes is best)

* means "cadence drill" (4-8) done every Wednesday
** means acceleration-glider drill, embedded in the run for that day (4-8)
*** means hills: after a 10 minute easy warm-up and 4 acceleration-gliders, run at 10K pace up a 150-200 yard hill. Walk down. No sprinting. See chapters 15 and 16 on hill running.

CROSS-COUNTRY RUNNING

Mon	Tues	Wed*	Thu	Fri ***	Sat	Sun
Week 1						
15-30 min ** then 2 hills	off/XT	18-40 min	off/XT	22-40 min	off	1.5-3 mi
Week 2**						
25-30 min ** then 3 hills	off/XT	28-45 min	off/XT	32- 45 min	off	2-4 mi
Week 3**						
30 min ** then 4 hills	off/XT	35-50 min	off/XT		off	3-4.5 mi
Week 4**						
Run 30 min ** then 5 hills	off/XT	42-55 min	off or XT		off	3-5 mi

CHAPTER 6

TRAINING ELEMENTS

Before beginning the following schedule, increase the long run to the distance of the first long one on the schedule. The other runs should also be a minimum of 30 minutes, twice a week. For at least two weeks before the start of any of these programs, insert 2-4 acceleration-gliders as noted by ** on the schedule. It helps to have done the cadence drill (*) for at least two weeks also. See chapter 14 for simple instructions on how to do these drills.

EVERY OTHER DAY?

If you are already running more than 3 days a week, and are not experiencing any fatigue or injury issues, you can certainly continue with the number of days that work into your schedule. Be careful, however. Speed training and the test days in this program will stress your muscles, tendons and motivation more than ever. When in doubt, back off and use the following schedule. If you are running more than three days a week, make sure that you take it very easy between each speed session. I strongly suggest that you take a day off or a very easy day before the "test day" and before the speed workout day.

CHANGING THE SPECIFIC WORKOUT DAYS

It's fine to shift the days around to accommodate races, team workouts and other activities. Try to take the day off before a long run or weekend race.

HOW SLOW FOR THE LONG RUNS—AND HOW OFTEN THE WALK BREAKS

Long runs should be run at least 3 min/mi slower than your current per mile race pace, or the predicted race pace, using the Prediction Time Trial. Feel free to run slower than this.

WALK BREAKS ON LONG RUNS

Even veterans will benefit from taking walk breaks during long runs. Each walk erases fatigue and will ease the feet and legs into running. During the early season, liberal use of walk breaks can virtually eliminate injuries normally produced on long runs. During the regular season walk breaks can speed up recovery. Here are the current run-walk-run strategies based upon pace per mile. There is a run-walk-run interval timer available at *www.JeffGalloway.com.*

Pace/mile	Run-Walk-Run strategy
8 min/mile	run 4 min/walk 30 seconds
8:30 min/mile	run 3 min/walk 30 seconds
9 min/mile	run 2 min/walk 30 seconds
9:30 min/mile	run 1:45-2 min/walk 30 seconds
10 min/mile	run 90 seconds/walk 30 seconds
10:30 min/mile	run 75 seconds/walk 30 seconds
11 min/mile	run 75-60 seconds/walk 30 seconds
12 min/mile	run 60 seconds/walk 30 seconds
13 min/mile	run 30 seconds/walk 30 seconds or 20/20
14 min/mile	30/30 or 20/20 or 15/15 or run 20/walk 30
15 min/mile	run 15 seconds/walk 30 seconds
16 min/mile	run 10 seconds/walk 30 seconds

WARM UP (AND WARM DOWN) BEFORE TEST DAYS AND SPEED DAY WORKOUTS

Here is a format that will get your mind and body ready to go faster. As you go through the training, fine-tune this to work for your specific needs. Then use the final product as your warm-up before the goal race.

The warm-down should be a reversal of the warm-up. Never go from a fast repetition into the car or the shower.

1. Walk slowly for 5 minutes.

2. Run a minute and walk a minute for 10 minutes.

3. Jog slowly for 10 minutes.

4. Walk for 3-4 minutes.

5. Do a cadence drill (4-8 of them).

6. Walk for 1-3 minutes.

7. Do an acceleration-glider drill (4-8).

8. Walk for 5 minutes.

9. Start the workout

PREDICTION TIME TRIALS (PTT)

These are your "reality checks" on your goal. Every other week you will run a timed race at 800 meters or 1 mile. You may take walk breaks or not on these time trials. The first one should not be run at an "all-out" effort. Your goal on each PTT after the first one is to run faster on each. Most runners tend to improve on each PTT, as the training effect improves performance. With each improvement, a faster time is predicted in the goal race. Coaches will often move athletes to a faster pace group based upon the PTT improvement.

If your predictions are a few seconds slower than your goal time, it's OK to continue with your current speed training program unless you are straining and/or breaking down with aches and pains. A safe strategy in the goal race is to start the race at the pace predicted by the average of your last two prediction time trials.

TEST RACE WORKOUTS (WO)

Coaches should group runners according to current conditioning level. Each "pace group" works together to bring each member through the workout, learning the best way to do so in the race itself. The first segment should be run as close to goal race pace as possible, on a smooth course that is measured. Walk for at least 5 minutes (no more than 10 minutes) and then do the second segment, trying to run about 1-2 seconds per quarter mile faster than goal pace. It is best to run these on a grass or dirt segment if there is little risk of injury due to uneven surface. Otherwise, pick a stable surface—even if it is a track or road. Some teams have the new/comeback runners run on track or pavement and the veterans run on stable cross-country terrain.

TEAM RUNNING

During speed workouts, teams can develop successful strategies for races. The power of the group pulls lazy runners out, helps those with low motivation to finish hard workouts and sets up a blueprint for race day. When pace groups are organized according to current ability levels, injuries are reduced. Many runners who need more confidence can often find it when running with a group. The Prediction Time Trial (PTT) can help sort runners into these groups. By running a faster time in the PTT, he or she can earn placement into the next pace group.

SPEED DAYS

Warm up well for these as noted in the speed section. Each of these speed segments should be run 5-7 seconds faster than you want to run a quarter of a mile in the goal race. Walk for 2-3 minutes between each quarter mile segment and repeat the process. In other words, take the per-mile pace you want to run in your goal race, divide it by 4, and subtract 5-7 seconds. Example: your goal pace is 6 minutes per mile: 6 divided by 4 = 1.5 or 1:30 per quarter mile. Subtracting 7 seconds means that your workout pace per quarter mile (or 400 meters) is 1:23. It is best that beginners do the speed workouts on the track. This tends to improve pace judgement.

NOTE: Gradually increase the speed on the faster workouts. Don't compete with the other runners during the workouts—save these resources for the races. Be sensitive to all "weak link" areas and cut back according to the advice in the injury section of this book.

HILLS

On Thursdays, after a very easy 10-minute warm-up, run the number of hills noted on the schedule. Don't sprint. Start each hill gently for about 3-6 strides, then pick up the pace due mostly to an increase in the cadence or "steps per minute." Keep shortening the stride to increase turnover as one runs up the hill. Work on a fast but smooth pace using a light touch of the foot. Beginner/comebackers should walk down the hill. Veterans should jog easily down the hill and walk for 1-2 minutes before starting the next one.

- Beginner/comebackers: hills approximately 60-100 yards long

- Veterans: hills approximately 200 yards long

- Advanced veterans: 300-400 yards long

LONG RUNS

If there are races scheduled on the weekends slated for longer long runs (LR), the remaining distance of the assigned long run can be run after the race at a very slow pace. Long runs can also be run on Sunday, after a Saturday race. In order to recover fast, to be ready for the speed training on Monday, athletes must run at least 3 min slower than current race pace, with very liberal walk breaks.

5K TRAINING PROGRAM: BEGINNER OR COMEBACK RUNNERS

CD = Cadence Drill

Acg = Acceleration-Glider

XT = Cross-Training (water running is best)

HT = Hill Training

PTT = Prediction Time Trial—1 mile

Standard warm-up: Walk 3 minutes, then 6 minutes run 1 minute/walk 20-30 seconds, then jog for 4 minutes slowly.

Standard warm down: Jog for 4 minutes very slowly, then 6 minutes run 1 minute/walk 20 seconds, then walk for 5 minutes.

Goal Pace: Confer with your coach about this. Most runners improve between 3-5% in a season.

WEEK 1

Monday: Standard warm-up then 4 cadence drills (CD), 2 acceleration-gliders (Acg). Remember, no sprinting! Then, a timed Prediction Time Trial (PTT) (one mile). Run at an easy pace for the first half and speed up a little during the second half. Don't sprint or compete with the runners around you on this PTT. The goal today is just to record a time for the mile, under control. Coaches can use the PTT times to sort runners into groups. Standard warm-down, afterward. The track is the best venue for this, to limit the variables and develop pace judgement.

Tuesday: Those who are just starting should take the day off from running. Cross-training (XT) is recommended (10-15 minutes of pool running is best). Runners who did the preseason training could jog a very easy 10-15 minutes or cross-train.

Wednesday: Speed day. This is the first speed workout so don't run this one fast. Standard warm-up, then 4 CDs and 3 Acgs (no sprinting). Then, run 3 x 400 (or .25 mi) at current race pace for 5K or slower. The purpose of this workout is to be gentle in adapting to faster running. Walk for 3 minutes between each. Then, use the standard warmdown. During the first 3 weeks, a track is best for this workout to learn pace judgment.

Thursday: 2 Hills (HT). Standard warm-up, then 3 Acgs. Next, run up a hill that is 60-100 yards long. Start each hill with 4-5 strides at a jog and gradually pick up the cadence of your feet. Shorten the stride as you ascend the hill, so that your leg motion feels smooth, with no straining. Glide slightly over the top of the hill and walk down gently, then do the second hill. Afterwards, do a standard warm-down. It is OK to run this workout on the same type of terrain that will be used in the races, as long as the footing is stable. Those with unstable ankles should run their hills on streets for at least the first 2-3 weeks.

Friday: Off—you've earned a day of rest.

Saturday: Race or long run of 2-3 miles.

- Racers should not run even close to "all-out." Take it very easy during the first mile. Many runners have found that a short walk break of 20-30 seconds, about every 4-5 minutes, helps them run faster than when running continuously. Don't sprint at the end—try to hold your position. Only those who did the preseason training should be racing hard at this point in the season. If this was your first week of training it is best to do the long run instead.

- If you're doing a long run (2-3 miles), be sure to read the pace guidelines (3 min/mi slower than race pace), and take the appropriate walk breaks, based upon pace per mile. Those who did not do the preseason training should use a run-walk-run ratio of "run a minute/walk a minute".

Sunday: Take the day off!

WEEK 2

Monday: Standard warm-up, 5 CDs, 3 Acgs (no sprinting). Then, run a timed mile at goal pace. Don't start too fast. Try to run each lap (or .25 mile) at the same pace. Walk for 5 minutes and run a 400 (or .25 mi) at race pace. Then do a standard warm-down. During the first 3 weeks of the season, it's best to run on the track to learn pace judgment. Don't run at a level that is causing pain. Standard warm-down.

Tuesday: Those who are just starting should take the day off from running. Fifteen to twenty minutes of XT is recommended (pool running is best). Runners who did the preseason training could jog a very easy 20 minutes or cross-train.

Wednesday: Speed day. This is the second speed workout so don't run this one too fast. Standard warm-up, then 4 CDs and 3 Acgs (no sprinting). Then, run 6 x 400 (or .25 mi) at current race pace for 5K or slower. The purpose of this workout is to be gentle in adapting to faster running. Walk for 3 minutes between each. Then, use the standard warm-down. During the first 3 weeks, a track is best for this workout to learn pace judgment.

Thursday: 3 Hills (HT). Standard warm-up, then 3 Acgs. Then, run up a hill that is 60-100 yards long. Start each hill with 4-5 strides at a jog and gradually pick up the cadence of your feet. Shorten the stride as you ascend the hill, so that your leg motion feels smooth, with no straining. Glide slightly over the top of the hill and walk for 2 minutes. Then run gently down the hill with a short to medium stride down and "coast" for about 50 yards on the flat (practicing a relaxed running form). Don't race other runners, and fine-tune your own downhill technique as you stay under control. Don't let the stride get too long. Walk for 2 minutes and repeat the cycle. Afterwards, do a standard warm-down. It is OK to run this workout on the same type of terrain that will be used in the races, as long as the footing is stable. Those with unstable ankles should run hills on streets.

Friday: Off—you've earned a day of rest.

Saturday: Race or long run of 3-3.5 miles.

- If this is the first race of the season, don't push into an "all-out" effort. Take it very easy during the first mile. If this is the second race of the season, you could run a little faster during the second half than in the first race. Many runners have found that a short walk break of 20-30 seconds, about every 4-5 minutes, helps them run faster than when running continuously—with more strength at the end. Don't sprint at the end, but you can gradually pick up the pace during the last mile.

- If you're doing a long run (3-3.5 miles), be sure to read the pace guidelines, and take the appropriate walk breaks, based upon pace per mile. You cannot go too slowly on the long run.

Sunday: If there are no significant aches and pains, jog easily for 10-15 minutes or take the day off!

WEEK 3

Monday: Standard warm-up, 6 CDs 4 Acgs (no sprinting). Then, a timed PTT (one mile). Your goal is to beat the time run in the first week. Pace yourself so that each lap (or .25 mile) is a little faster than the same unit on the first PTT. Don't sprint or compete with other runners on this PTT. Standard warm-down. The track is the best venue for the PTT. Look at the tables in chapter 4 to see what your potential is currently in an ideal 5K on the track. This will allow you to start focusing on a goal. (Cross-country times tend to be slower than track times, for the same distance.)

Tuesday: 20 to 30 minutes of XT is recommended (pool running is best). Runners who did the preseason training could jog a very easy 20 minutes or cross-train.

Wednesday: Speed day. Standard warm-up, then 5 CDs and 4 Acgs (no sprinting). Then, run 8 x 400 (or .25 mi) about 1-2 seconds faster than current race pace for 5K. Walk for 3 minutes between each. Then, use the standard warm-down.

Thursday: 4 HTs. Standard warm-up, then 3 Acgs. Then, run up a hill that is 60-100 yards long. Start each hill with 4-5 strides at a jog and gradually pick up the cadence of your feet. Shorten the stride as you ascend the hill, so that your leg motion feels smooth, with no straining. Glide slightly over the top of the hill and walk for 2 minutes. Then run gently down the hill with a short to medium stride, and "coast" out onto the flat for about 50 yards (practicing downhill running form). Don't race other runners, but fine-tune your own downhill technique as you stay under control. Don't let the stride get too long. Walk for 2 minutes and repeat the cycle. Afterwards, do a standard warm-down. It is OK to run this workout on the same type of terrain that will be run in the races, as long as the footing is stable. Those with unstable ankles should run hills on streets.

Friday: Off—you've earned a day of rest.

Saturday: Race or long run of 4 miles.

- Racers should not run at top speed or "all-out", but the pace could be increased from the last race. Take it easy during the first mile. Pick up it up a little in the second mile. On the third mile, pass a few runners. Many runners have found that a short walk break of 20-30 seconds, about every 4-5 minutes, helps them run faster than when running continuously. Don't sprint at the end, but you could gradually pick it up during the final 200 meters.

- If you're doing a long run, be sure to read the pace guidelines (three minutes per mile slower than race pace), and take the appropriate walk breaks, based upon pace per mile. You cannot run too slow on the long run.

- If you are racing every weekend, jog a very slow 1 mile after the race—with lots of walk breaks.

Sunday: If there are no significant aches and pains, jog easily for 15-20 minutes or take the day off!

WEEK 4

Monday: Standard warm-up, 6 CDs, 5 Acgs (no sprinting). Then, run 1.5 miles at goal pace. Don't start too fast. Try to run each lap (or .25 mile) at the same pace. Walk for 5 minutes and run 2 x 400 (or .25 mi ea) about 2 seconds faster than race pace, but don't sprint! Walk half a lap between the 400s. Then do a standard warm-down. The track is still the best venue for this workout.

Tuesday: 20-30 minutes of XT is recommended (pool running is best). Runners who did the preseason training could jog a very easy 20-25 minutes or cross-train.

Wednesday: Speed day. Standard warm-up, then 5 CDs and 5 Acgs (no sprinting). Then, run 9 x 400 (or .25 mi). Run the first 2 x 400 about 5 seconds faster than current race pace for 5K. Walk for 3 minutes between each. Run the last 7 x 400s, about 3 seconds faster than current race pace. Then, use the standard warm-down. This could be run on an accurately measured cross-country course, with stable footing (or the track).

Thursday: 4 HTs. Standard warm-up, then 3 Acgs. Then, run up a hill that is 60-100 yards long. Start each hill with 4-5 strides at a jog and gradually pick up the cadence of your feet. Shorten the stride as you ascend the hill, so that your leg motion feels smooth, with no straining. Glide slightly over the top of the hill and walk for 2 minutes. Then run gently down the hill with a short to medium stride, and "coast" out onto the flat for about 50 yards (practicing downhill running form). Don't race other runners, but fine-tune your own downhill technique as you stay under control. Don't let the stride get too long. Walk for 2 minutes and repeat the cycle. Afterwards, do a standard warm-down. It is OK to run this workout on the same type of terrain that will be running in the races, as long as the footing is stable. Those with unstable ankles should run hills on streets.

Friday: Off—you've earned a day of rest.

Saturday: Race or long run of 4 miles.

- Racers can start to run a little faster during the first 200 meters of the race (see chapter 13 on race strategies). Ease into a steady pace until the last half-mile of the race. During the last half-mile, try to pass one runner at a time. Don't sprint at the end, but you could gradually pick it up. No puking.

- If you're doing a long run (4 miles), be sure to read the pace guidelines (three minutes per mile slower than race pace), and take the appropriate walk breaks, based upon pace per mile. You cannot run too slowly on the long run.

- If you are racing every weekend, it will help to run very easily for 1.5 miles after the race, 3 min/mi slower than race pace.

Sunday: If there are no significant aches and pains, jog easily for 30 minutes or take the day off!

WEEK 5

Monday: Standard warm-up, 6 CDs, 5 Acgs (no sprinting). Then, a timed PTT (one mile). Your goal is to beat the best PTT so far. Pace yourself so that each lap (or .25 mile) is a little faster than the same unit on the best effort so far. Start to push yourself a little on the last lap without sprinting. The track is best for the PTT—to provide an accurate time comparison. Look at the tables in chapter 4 to see what your potential is currently in an ideal 5K on the track. This will allow you to continue focusing on a goal. Talk this over with the coach.

Tuesday: 20-30 minutes of XT is recommended (pool running is best). Runners who did the preseason training could jog a very easy 20 minutes or cross-train.

Wednesday: Speed day. Standard warm-up, then 5 CDs and 5 Acgs (no sprinting). Then, run 11 x 400 (or .25 mi). Run the first 2 x 400 about 5 seconds faster than current race pace for 5K. Walk for 3 minutes between each. Run the last 9 x 400s, about 3 seconds faster than current race pace. Then, use the standard warm-down. This could be run on an accurately measured cross-country course, with stable footing (or the track).

Thursday: 4 HTs. Standard warm-up, then 3 Acgs. Then, run up a hill that is 60-100 yards long. Start each hill with 4-5 strides at a jog and gradually pick up the cadence of your feet. Shorten the stride as you ascend the hill, so that your leg motion feels smooth, with no straining. Glide slightly over the top of the hill and walk for 2 minutes. Then run gently down the hill with a short to medium stride, and "coast" out onto the flat for about 50 yards (practicing downhill running form). Don't race other runners, but fine-tune your own downhill technique as you stay under control. Don't let the stride get too long. Walk for 2 minutes and repeat the cycle. Afterwards, do a standard warm-down. It is OK to run this workout on the same type of terrain that will be running in the races, as long as the footing is stable. Those with unstable ankles should run hills on streets.

Friday: Off—you've earned a day of rest.

Saturday: Race or long run of 4.5-5 miles.

- Racers should practice running a little faster during the first 200 meters of the race to get away from the mass of the crowd (see chapter 13 on race strategy). Ease into a steady pace until the last half-mile of the race. During the last half-mile, try to pass one runner at a time. Don't sprint at the end, but you could gradually pick it up. No puking.

- If you're doing a long run (4.5 to 5 miles), be sure to read the pace guidelines (three minutes per mile slower than race pace), and take the appropriate walk breaks, based upon pace per mile. You cannot run too slowly on the long run.

- If you are racing every weekend, it will help to run very easily for 1.5 miles after the race, 3 min/mi slower than race pace.

Sunday: If there are no significant aches and pains, jog easily for 30 minutes or take the day off!

WEEK 6

Monday: Standard warm-up, 6 CDs, 6 Acgs (no sprinting). Then, run 2 miles at goal pace. It's OK to start a little faster than goal pace to get ready to run a little faster at the start of your cross-country races. Try to run each lap (or .25 mile) at the same pace. Walk for 5 minutes and run 2 x 400 (or .25 mi ea) about 2 seconds faster than race pace, but don't sprint! Walk half a lap between each. Then do a standard warm-down.

Tuesday: 20-30 minutes of XT is recommended (pool running is best). Runners who did the preseason training could jog a very easy 20 minutes or cross-train.

Wednesday: Speed day. Standard warm-up, then 5 CDs and 5 Acgs (no sprinting). Then, run 13 x 400 (or .25 mi). Run the first 2 x 400 about 5 seconds faster than current race pace for 5K. Walk for 3 minutes between each. Run the last 11 x 400s, about 3 seconds faster than current race pace. Then, use the standard warm-down. This could be run on an accurately measured cross-country course, with stable footing (or the track).

Thursday: 4 HTs. Standard warm-up, then 3 acceleration gliders. Then, run up a hill that is 60-100 yards long. Start each hill with 4-5 strides at a jog and gradually pick up the cadence of your feet. Shorten the stride as you ascend the hill, so that your leg motion feels smooth, with no straining. Glide slightly over the top of the hill and walk for 2 minutes. Then run gently down the hill with a short to medium stride, and "coast" out onto the flat for about 50 yards (practicing downhill running form). Don't race other runners, but fine-tune your own downhill technique as you stay under control. Don't let the stride get too long. Walk for 2 minutes and repeat the cycle. Afterwards, do a standard warm-down. It is OK to run this workout on the same type of terrain that will be running in the races, as long as the footing is stable. Those with unstable ankles should run hills on streets.

Friday: Off—you've earned a day of rest.

Saturday: Race or long run of 5-6.5 miles.

- Racers can start to run a little faster during the first 200 meters of the race (see chapter 13 on race strategies. Ease into a steady pace until the last half-mile of the race. During the last mile, try to pass one runner at a time. Don't sprint at the end, but you could gradually pick it up. No puking.

- If you're doing a long run (5-6.5 miles), be sure to read the pace guidelines (three minutes per mile slower than race pace), and take the appropriate walk breaks, based upon pace per mile. You cannot run too slowly on the long run.

- If you are racing every weekend, it will help to run very easily for 2-3 miles after the race, 3 min/mi slower than race pace. Use lots of walk breaks (even 1 min run/1 min walk if needed).

Sunday: If there are no significant aches and pains, jog easily for 30 minutes or take the day off!

WEEK 7 GOAL RACE WEEK

Monday: Standard warm-up, 6 CDs, 6 Acgs (no sprinting). Talk strategy with teammates and start the workout. If possible, run on the race course or similar terrain. Run the first half-mile a little faster than goal pace, practicing race strategy. Try to run the second half-mile at goal pace. This is race practice and not competition–don't run too fast. Walk for 5 minutes and run 2 x 400 (or .25 mi ea) at about race pace. Walk about 200 meters between each. Then do a standard warm-down.

Tuesday: This should be a very easy day or a day off. XT is recommended (pool running is best for 20 minutes).

Wednesday: Speed day. This is the last speed workout before the first goal race, so save the effort for the race. Standard warm-up, then 5 CDs and 5 Acgs (no sprinting). Then, run 4 x 400 (or .25 mi) about 2-3 seconds faster than current race pace for 5K. Walk for 3 minutes between each. Then, use the standard warm-down. This can be run on cross-country terrain.

Thursday: 2 HTs. Standard warm-up, then 4 Acgs. Don't push the effort on this workout—run for technique only. Run up each hill (60-100 yards long). Start each hill with 4-5 strides at a jog and gradually pick up the cadence of your feet. Shorten the stride as you ascend the hill, so that your leg motion feels smooth, with no straining. Glide slightly over the top of the hill and jog down gently. Afterwards, do a standard warm-down.

Friday: Off—rest for the race.

Saturday: Race!

- Racers should use the techniques that have worked well before, working with teammates when possible. Start just fast enough to get ahead of the bulk of the runners, but not so fast to leave the muscles exhausted during the last mile. Read chapter 13 on race strategy. During the second mile, try to pass one runner at a time to the finish. Don't save up for a final sprint—gradually pick it up during the last mile.

Sunday: If there are no significant aches and pains, jog easily for 30 minutes or take the day off!

- If you are running more races, alternate weeks 6 and 7.

- If the season is over, congratulations. Enjoy running every other day or start training for another goal.

CHAPTER 8

5K TRAINING PROGRAM: VETERAN RUNNERS/TIME IMPROVEMENT

CD = Cadence Drill

Acg = Acceleration-Glider

XT = Cross-Training (water running is best)

HT = Hill Training (100-200 yds long)

PTT = Prediction Time Trial—1 mile (if a measured segment is used, use the same one each time)

Standard warm-up: Walk 3 minutes, then 6 minutes of slow jogging, then run at a normal easy day running pace.

Standard warm-down: Jog for 4 minutes of running at a normal easy day running pace, then 10 minutes of very slow running, then walk for 4 minutes.

Goal Pace: Confer with your coach about this. Most runners improve between 3-5% in a season.

NOTE: Only veterans who have done the preseason training should use this program. Otherwise, use the "Comeback" 5K program.

WEEK 1

Monday: Standard warm-up, 4 cadence drills (CD), 2 acceleration-gliders (Acg). Remember, no sprinting! Then, a timed Prediction Time Trial (PTT) (one mile). Run at an easy pace for the first half and speed up a little during the second half. Don't sprint or compete with the runners around you on this PTT. The goal today is just to record a time for the mile, under control. Coaches can use the PTT times to sort runners into groups. Standard warm-down afterward. The track is the best venue for this to limit the variables and develop pace judgment.

Tuesday: Those who have just restarted their training should take the day off from running, or jog for 10-15 minutes. Cross-training (XT) is recommended (15 minutes of pool running is best). Runners who did all of the preseason training could jog a very easy 30 minutes or cross-train.

Wednesday: Speed day. This is the first speed workout so warm up well and don't run the first few repetitions too fast. Standard warm-up, then 4 CDs and 3 Acgs (no sprinting). Then, run 2 x 800 (or half a mile) at current race pace for 5K. The purpose of this workout is to be gentle in adapting to faster running. Walk for 3 minutes between each. Then, use the standard warm-down. During the first week, a track or a flat and stable surface best for this workout.

Thursday: 2 Hills (HT). Standard warm-up, then 3 Acgs. Then, run up a hill that is 100-150 yards long. Start each hill with 4-5 strides at a jog and gradually pick up the cadence of your feet. Shorten the stride as you ascend the hill, so that your leg motion feels smooth, with no straining. Glide slightly over the top of the hill and walk down gently, then do the second hill. Afterwards, do a standard warm-down. It is OK to run this workout on the same type of terrain that will be used in the races, as long as the footing is stable. Those with unstable ankles should run their hills on streets (or other stable terrain) for at least the first 2-3 weeks.

Friday: Off—you've earned a day of rest.

Saturday: Race or one mile time trial.

- Racers should not run even close to "all-out." Take it very easy during the first mile. Don't sprint at the end—try to hold your position. Only those who did the preseason training should be racing hard at this point in the season. Those who did not do the full preseason training could run an easy race this week.

Sunday: 4 miles (at least 3 min/mi slower than current 5K race pace). Be sure to insert walk breaks as noted in chapter 18. The long runs cannot be run too slowly. Running a bit too fast on long runs is a primary cause of injury.

WEEK 2

Monday: Standard warm-up, 5 CDs, 3 Acgs (no sprinting). Then, run a timed mile at goal pace. Don't start too fast. Try to run each lap (or .25 mile) at the same pace. Walk and jog for 5 minutes and run half a mile (or 800 meters) at race pace or slightly faster. This could be run on "cross-country terrain" as long as the footing is stable. Standard warm-down.

Tuesday: Run very easy for 3 miles, or do 20-30 minutes of XT. Running in the deep end of the pool can help one run smoother. It is fine to both run and cross-train. Save the effort for Wednesday's workout.

Wednesday: Speed day (3 x 800 meter). This is the second speed workout and your body is still adjusting to fast running. Warm up well and don't run the first repetition too fast. Standard warm-up, then 4 CDs and 3 Acgs (no sprinting). Next, run the first 800 (or half a mile) at current race pace for 5K. Walk and jog for 3 minutes and repeat. Run two more 800s, slightly faster than race pace. Then, use the standard warm-down. You can run on the same type of terrain as that used in races—as long as the surface is stable.

Thursday: 4 HTs. Standard warm-up, then 3 Acgs. Then, run up a hill that is 150-200 yards long. Start each hill with 4-5 strides at a jog and gradually pick up the cadence of your feet. Shorten the stride as you ascend the hill, so that your leg motion feels smooth, with no straining. Glide slightly over the top of the hill and walk for 2 minutes. Then run gently down the hill with a short to medium stride down and "coast" for about 50 yards on the flat (practicing a relaxed running form). Don't race other runners, and fine-tune your own downhill technique as you stay under control. Don't let the stride get too long. Walk for 2 minutes and repeat the cycle. Afterwards, do a standard warm-down. It is OK to run this workout on the same type of terrain that will be used in the races, as long as the footing is stable. Those with unstable ankles should run hills on streets. Don't test yourself on this workout—fine-tune your running form.

Friday: Off—you've earned a day of rest.

Saturday: Race or long run of 5.5 miles.

- If this is the first race of the season, don't push into an "all-out" effort. Take it very easy during the first mile. If this is the second race of the season, you could run a little faster during the second half than in the first race. Don't sprint at the end, but you can gradually pick up the pace during the last mile.

- If you're doing a long run (5.5 miles), be sure to read the pace guidelines, and take the appropriate walk breaks, based upon pace per mile. You cannot go too slowly on the long run.

- If you had a race this weekend, run an additional 2.5 miles after the race, running 3 min/mi slower than race pace—or slower.

Sunday: If there are no significant aches and pains, jog easily for 10-15 minutes or take the day off!

WEEK 3

Monday: Standard warm-up, 6 CDs, 4 ACgs (no sprinting). Then, a timed PTT (one mile). Your goal is to beat the time run in the first week. Pace yourself so that each lap (or .25 mile) is a little faster than the same unit on the first PTT. Don't sprint or compete with other runners on this PTT. Standard warm-down. After the PTT, run 3 x 400 at goal race pace, jogging 200 meters between each. The track is the best venue for the PTT. Look at the tables in chapter 4 to see what your potential is currently in an ideal 5K on the track (multiply the mile time by 3.4). Talk to your coach about your goal for the upcoming races. (Cross-country times tend to be slower than track times, for the same distance.)

Tuesday: 20 to 30 minutes of XT is recommended (pool running is best). Runners who did the preseason training could jog a very easy 20 minutes or cross-train.

Wednesday: Speed day. Standard warm-up, then 5 CDs and 4 Acgs (no sprinting). Then, run 4 x 800 (half mile) about 4-5 seconds faster than current goal pace for 5K. Start running a little faster during the first 200 meters, then assuming workout pace for the rest. Walk/jog slowly for 3 minutes between each. Then, use the standard warm-down. Cross-country race terrain is best for this workout as long as the surface is stable.

Thursday: 4 HTs. Standard warm-up, then 4 Acgs. Then, run up a hill that is 150-250 yards long. Start each hill with 4-5 strides at a jog and gradually pick up the cadence of your feet. Shorten the stride as you ascend the hill, so that your leg motion feels smooth, with no straining. Glide slightly over the top of the hill and walk for 2 minutes. Then run gently down the hill with a short to medium stride, and "coast" out onto the flat for about 50 yards (practicing downhill running form). Don't race other runners, but fine-tune your own downhill technique as you stay under control. Don't let the stride get too long. Walk for 2 minutes and repeat the cycle. Afterwards, do a standard warm-down. It is OK to run this workout on the same type of terrain that will be run in the races, as long as the footing is stable. Those with unstable ankles should run hills on streets.

Friday: Off—you've earned a day of rest.

Saturday: Race or long run of 7 miles.

- Racers should go out a little faster than they have been running, for the first 200 meters. Then maintain a good pace, but not too fast for the first mile. Pick up the pace a little in the second mile. On the third mile, pass a few runners. Don't sprint at the end, but you could gradually pick it up during the final half mile.

- If you're doing a long run, be sure to read the pace guidelines (three minutes per mile slower than race pace), and take the appropriate walk breaks, based upon pace per mile. You cannot run too slow on the long run.

- If you are racing this weekend, jog a very slow 4 miles after the race (3 min/mi slower than current race pace)—with lots of walk breaks.

Sunday: If there are no significant aches and pains, jog easily for 15-20 minutes or take the day off!

WEEK 4

Monday: Standard warm-up, 6 CDs, 5 Acgs (no sprinting). Then, run 1.5 miles at goal pace. Don't start too fast. Try to run each lap (or .25 mile) at the same pace. Walk for 5 minutes and run 3 x 400 (or .25 mi ea) about 2 seconds faster than race pace, but don't sprint! Walk half a lap between the 400s. Then do a standard warm-down. Cross-country terrain is best for this workout—as long as the surface is stable.

Tuesday: 20-30 minutes of XT is recommended (pool running is best). Runners who did the preseason training could jog a very easy 20-25 minutes or cross-train.

Wednesday: Speed day. Standard warm-up, then 5 CDs and 5 Acgs (no sprinting). Then, run 5 x 800 (half mile). Run the first 2 x 800 about 8 seconds faster than goal race pace for 5K. During the first 200 meters of each 800, run a little faster than workout pace. Walk/jog for 3 minutes between each. Run the last 3 x 800s, about 5 seconds faster than current race pace. Then, use the standard warm-down. The best venue is an accurately measured cross-country course, with stable footing (or the track).

Thursday: 4 HIs. Standard warm-up, then 4 Acgs. Then, run up a hill that is 200-300 yards long. Start each hill with 4-5 strides at a jog and gradually pick up the cadence of your feet. Shorten the stride as you ascend the hill, so that your leg motion feels smooth, with no straining. Glide slightly over the top of the hill and walk for 2 minutes. Then run gently down the hill with a short to medium stride, and "coast" out onto the flat for about 50 yards (practicing downhill running form). Don't race other runners, but fine-tune your own downhill technique as you stay under control. Don't let the stride get too long. Walk for 2 minutes and repeat the cycle. Afterwards, do a standard warm-down. It is OK to run this workout on the same type of terrain that will be run in the races, as long as the footing is stable. Those with unstable ankles should run hills on streets.

Friday: Off—you've earned a day of rest.

Saturday: Race or long run of 8.5 miles.

- Racers can start to run a little faster during the first 200 meters of the race (see chapter 13 on race strategies). After the first mile, try a strategy of catching up with the next group ahead, running with them for 100-200 yards, then passing and gradually moving on to the next group or individual. Ease into a steady pace until the last half-mile of the race. During the last half-mile, try to pass one runner at a time. Don't sprint at the end, but you could gradually pick it up. No puking.

- If you're doing a long run (8.5 miles), be sure to read the pace guidelines (three minutes per mile slower than race pace), and take the appropriate walk breaks, based upon pace per mile. You cannot run too slowly on the long run.

- If you are racing every weekend, it will help to run very easily for 5.5 miles after the race, 3 min/mi slower than race pace. It is also possible to do a warm-down after the race and run the slow long run on Sunday.

Sunday: If there are no significant aches and pains, jog easily for 30 minutes or take the day off!

WEEK 5

Monday: Standard warm-up, 6 CDs, 5 Acgs (no sprinting). Then, a timed PTT (one mile). Your goal is to beat the best PTT so far. Pace yourself so that each lap (or .25 mile) is a little faster than the same unit on the best effort so far. Start to push yourself a little on the last lap without sprinting. Walk for 5 minutes and do 3 x 400, 2 seconds faster than race pace, jogging 200 between each The track is best for the PTT—to provide an accurate time comparison. Look at the tables in chapter 4 to see what your potential is currently in an ideal 5K on the track (multiply the mile time by 3.4). Talk to your coach about your goal for the upcoming races.

Tuesday: 20-30 minutes of XT is recommended (pool running is best). Runners who did the preseason training could jog a very easy 20 minutes or cross-train. If you run today, save the effort for Wednesday's workout.

Wednesday: Speed day. Standard warm-up, then 5 CDs and 5 Acgs (no sprinting). Then, run 6 x 800 (half mile). Run the first 2 x 800 about 8 seconds faster than goal race pace for 5K. During the first 200 meters of each 800, run a little faster than workout pace to practice running fast at the beginning of the race. Walk/jog for 3 minutes between each. Run the last 4 x 800s, about 5 seconds faster than current race pace. Then, use the standard warm-down. This could be run on an accurately measured cross-country course, with stable footing (or the track).

Thursday: 4 HTs. Standard warm-up, then 3 Acgs. Then, run up a hill that is 200-300 yards long. Start each hill with 4-5 strides at a jog and gradually pick up the cadence of your feet. Shorten the stride as you ascend the hill, so that your leg motion feels smooth, with no straining. Glide slightly over the top of the hill and walk for 2 minutes. Then run gently down the hill with a short to medium stride, and "coast" out onto the flat for about 50 yards (practicing downhill running form). Don't race other runners, but fine-tune your own downhill technique as you stay under control. Don't let the stride get too long. Walk for 2 minutes and repeat the cycle. Afterwards, do a standard warm-down. It is OK to run this workout on the same type of terrain that will be run in the races, as long as the footing is stable. Those with unstable ankles should run hills on streets.

Friday: Off—you've earned a day of rest.

Saturday: Race or long run of 10 miles.

- Racers can start to run a little faster during the first 200 meters of the race (see chapter 13 on race strategies). After the first mile, try a strategy of catching up with the next group ahead, running with them for 100-200 yards, then passing for the next group or individual. Ease into a steady pace until the last half-mile of the race. During the last half-mile, try to pass one runner at a time. Don't sprint at the end, but you could gradually pick it up. No puking.

- If you're doing a long run (10 miles), be sure to read the pace guidelines (three minutes per mile slower than race pace), and take the appropriate walk breaks, based upon pace per mile. You cannot run too slowly on the long run.

- If you are racing this weekend, run very easily for 7 miles after the race, 3 min/mi slower than race pace. You could also run this long run on Sunday—going even slower than usual.

Sunday: If there are no significant aches and pains, jog easily for 30 minutes or take the day off!

WEEK 6

Monday: Standard warm-up, 6 CDs, 6 Acgs (no sprinting). Then, run 2 miles at goal pace. It's OK to start a little faster than goal pace to get ready to prepare for running a little faster at the start of your cross-country races. Try to run each lap (or .25 mile) at the same pace. Work together with other runners at your pace, pulling one another along. Walk for 5 minutes and run 2 x 400 (or .25 mi each) about 2 seconds faster than race pace, but don't sprint! Walk half a lap between each. Then do a standard warm-down.

Tuesday: 20-30 minutes of XT is recommended (pool running is best). About 20 minutes of easy running is also OK if the legs are not too tired from Monday's workout. Take it easy today to prepare for Wednesday's workout.

Wednesday: Speed day. Standard warm-up, then 5 CDs and 5 Acgs (no sprinting). Then, run 7 x 800 (half mile). Run the first 2 x 800 about 8 seconds faster than goal race pace for 5K. During the first 200 meters of each 800, run a little faster than workout pace. Walk/jog for 3 minutes between each. Run the last 5 x 800s, about 5 seconds faster than current race pace. Then, use the standard warm-down. The best venue is an accurately measured cross-country course, with stable footing (or the track).

Thursday: 4 HTs. Standard warm-up, then 3 Acgs. Then, run up a hill that is 200-300 yards long. Start each hill with 4-5 strides at a jog and gradually pick up the cadence of your feet. Shorten the stride as you ascend the hill, so that your leg motion feels smooth, with no straining. Glide slightly over the top of the hill and walk for 2 minutes. Then run gently down the hill with a short to medium stride, and "coast" out onto the flat for about 50 yards (practicing downhill running form). Don't race other runners, but fine-tune your own downhill technique as you stay under control. Don't let the stride get too long. Walk for 2 minutes and repeat the cycle. Afterwards, do a standard warm-down. It is OK to run this workout on the same type of terrain that will be run in the races, as long as the footing is stable. Those with unstable ankles should run hills on streets.

Friday: Off—you've earned a day of rest.

Saturday: Race or long run of 6 miles.

- Racers can start to run a little faster during the first 200 meters of the race (see chapter 13 on race strategies). Talk over strategy with teammates before the race. After the first mile, try a strategy of catching up with the next group ahead, running with them for 100-200 yards, then passing for the next group or individual. Ease into a steady pace until the last half-mile of the race. During the last half-mile, try to pass one runner at a time. Don't sprint at the end, but you could gradually pick it up. Smile!

- If you're doing a long run (6 miles), be sure to read the pace guidelines (three minutes per mile slower than race pace), and take the appropriate walk breaks, based upon pace per mile. You cannot run too slowly on the long run

- If you are racing this weekend, run very easily for 3 miles after the race, 3 min/mi slower than race pace.

Sunday: If there are no significant aches and pains, jog easily for 30 minutes or take the day off!

WEEK 7 GOAL RACE WEEK

Monday: Standard warm-up, 6 CDs, 6 Acgs (no sprinting). Talk strategy with teammates and start the workout. If possible, run on the race course or similar terrain. Run the first half-mile a little faster than goal pace, practicing race strategy. Try to run the second half-mile at goal pace. This is race practice and not competition—don't run too fast. Walk for 5 minutes and run 2 x 400 (or .25 mi ea) at about race pace. Walk about 200 meters between each. Then do a standard warm-down.

Tuesday: This should be a very easy day or a day off. XT is recommended (pool running is best for 20 minutes).

Wednesday: Speed day. This is the last speed workout before the first goal race, so save the effort for the race. Standard warm-up, then 5 CDs and 5 Acgs (no sprinting). Then, run 4 x 400 (or .25 mi) about 2-3 seconds faster than current race pace for 5K. Walk for 3 minutes between each. Then, use the standard warm-down. This can be run on cross-country terrain.

Thursday: 2HTs. Standard warm-up, then 4 Acgs. Don't push the pace on these hills, just work on form and technique. Run up each hill (11-150 yards long). Start each hill with 4-5 strides at a jog and gradually pick up the cadence of your feet. Shorten the stride as you ascend the hill, so that your leg motion feels smooth, with no straining. Glide slightly over the top of the hill and jog down gently. Afterwards, do a standard warm-down.

Friday: Off—rest for the race.

Saturday: Race!

- Racers should use the techniques that have worked well before, working with teammates when possible. Start just fast enough to get ahead of the bulk of the runners, but not so fast to leave the muscles exhausted during the last mile. Read chapter 13 on race strategies. During the second mile, try to pass one runner at a time to the finish. Don't save up for a final sprint—gradually pick it up during the last mile.

Sunday: If there are no significant aches and pains, jog easily for 30 minutes or take the day off!

- If you are running more races, alternate weeks 6 and 7.

- If the season is over, congratulations. Enjoy running every other day or start training for another goal.

CHAPTER 9

2 MILE TRAINING PROGRAM (ALSO 3000-3200 METERS): BEGINNER OR COMEBACK RUNNERS

CD = Cadence Drill

Acg – Acceleration-Glider

XT = Cross-Training (water running is best)

HT = Hill Training (60-150 yds long)

PTT = Prediction Time Trial—1 mile

Standard warm-up: Walk 3 minutes, then 6 minutes run 1 minute/walk 20 seconds, then jog for 4 minutes slowly.

Standard warm-down: Jog for 4 minutes very slowly, then 6 minutes run 1 minute/walk for 20 seconds, then walk for 5 minutes.

WEEK 1—PRIME MISSION: STAY INJURY-FREE

Monday: Standard warm-up, 4 cadence drills (CD), 2 acceleration-gliders (Acg). Remember, no sprinting! Then, a timed Prediction Time Trial (PTT) (one mile). Run at an easy pace for the first half and speed up a little during the second half. Don't sprint or compete with the runners around you on this PTT. The goal today is just to record a time for the mile, under control. Coaches can use the PTT times to sort runners into groups. Standard warm-down afterward. The track is the best venue for this to limit the variables and develop pace judgment.

Tuesday: Those who are just starting should take the day off from running. Cross- training (XT) is recommended (10-15 minutes of pool running is best). Runners who did the preseason training could jog a very easy 10-15 minutes or cross-train.

Wednesday: Speed day. This is the first speed workout so don't run this one fast. Standard warm-up, then 4 CDs and 3 Acgs (no sprinting). Then, run 2 x 400 (or .25 mi) at current race pace for 2 Mile or slower. The purpose of this workout is to be gentle in adapting to faster running. Walk for 3 minutes between each. Then, use the standard warm-down. During the first 3 weeks, at least, a track is best for this workout to learn pace judgment.

Thursday: 2 Hills (HT). Standard warm-up, then 3 Acgs. Then, run up a hill that is 60-80 yards long. Start each hill with 4-5 strides at a jog and gradually pick up the cadence of your feet. Shorten the stride as you ascend the hill, so that your leg motion feels smooth, with no straining. Glide slightly over the top of the hill and walk down gently, then do the second hill. Afterwards, do a standard warm-down. It is OK to run this workout on the same type of terrain that will be used in the races, as long as the footing is stable. Those with unstable ankles should run their hills on streets for at least the first 2-3 weeks.

Friday: Off—you've earned a day of rest.

Saturday: Race or long run of 2 miles.

- Racers should not run even close to "all-out." Take it very easy during the first mile. Many runners have found that a short walk break of 20-30 seconds, about every 4-5 minutes, helps them run faster than when running continuously. Don't sprint at the end—try to hold your position. Only those who did the preseason training should be racing hard at this point in the season. If this was your first week of training it is best to do the long run instead.

- If you're doing a long run (2 miles), be sure to read the pace guidelines (3 min/mi slower than race pace), and take the appropriate walk breaks, based upon pace per mile. Those who did not do the preseason training should use a run-walk-run of (run 1 minute/walk 1 minute).

Sunday: Take the day off!

WEEK 2

Monday: Standard warm-up, 5 CDs, 3 Acgs (no sprinting). Then, run a timed half- mile (or 800 meters) at goal pace. Don't start too fast. Try to run each lap (or .25 mile) at the same pace. Walk for 5 minutes and run a 400 (or .25 mi) at race pace. Then do a standard warm-down. During the first 3 weeks of the season, it's best to run on the track to learn pace judgment. Don't run at a level that is causing pain.

Tuesday: Those who are just starting should take the day off from running. Fifteen to twenty minutes of XT is recommended (pool running is best). Runners who did the preseason training could jog a very easy 20 minutes or cross-train.

Wednesday: Speed day. This is only the second speed workout so don't run this one too fast. Standard warm-up, then 4 CDs and 3 Acgs (no sprinting). Then, run 4 x 400 (or .25 mi) at current race pace for 2 Miles. The purpose of this workout is to be gentle in adapting to faster running. Walk for 3 minutes between each. Then, use the standard warmdown. During the first 3 weeks, a track is best for this workout to learn pace judgment.

Thursday: 3 HTs. Standard warm-up, then 3 Acgs. Then, run up a hill that is 60-80 yards long. Start each hill with 4-5 strides at a jog and gradually pick up the cadence of your feet. Shorten the stride as you ascend the hill, so that your leg motion feels smooth, with no straining. Glide slightly over the top of the hill and walk for 2 minutes. Then run gently down the hill with a short to medium stride down and "coast" for about 50 yards on the flat (practicing a relaxed running form). Don't race other runners, and fine-tune your own downhill technique as you stay under control. Don't let the stride get too long. Walk for 2 minutes and repeat the cycle. Afterwards, do a standard warm-down. It is OK to run this workout on the same type of terrain that will be used in the races, as long as the footing is stable. Those with unstable ankles should run hills on streets.

Friday: Off—you've earned a day of rest.

Saturday: Race or long run of 2.5 miles.

- If this is the first race of the season, don't push into an "all-out" effort. Take it very easy during the first mile. If this is the second race of the season, you could run a little faster during the second half than in the first race. Many runners have found that a short walk break of 20-30 seconds, about every 4-5 minutes, helps them run faster than when running continuously—with more strength at the end. Don't sprint at the end, but you can gradually pick up the pace during the last mile.

- If you're doing a long run (2.5 miles), be sure to read the pace guidelines, and take the appropriate walk breaks, based upon pace per mile. You cannot go too slowly on the long run.

Sunday: If there are no significant aches and pains, jog easily for 10-15 minutes or take the day off!

WEEK 3

Monday: Standard warm-up, 6 CDs, 4 Acgs (no sprinting). Then, a timed PTT (one mile). Your goal is to beat the time run in the first week. Pace yourself so that each lap (or .25 mile) is a little faster than the same unit on the first PTT. Don't sprint or compete with other runners on this PTT. Standard warm-down. The track is the best venue for the PTT. Look at the tables in chapter 4 to see what your potential is currently in an ideal 2 Mile on the track. This will allow you to start focusing on a goal. (Cross-country times tend to be slower than track times, for the same distance.)

Tuesday: 20 to 30 minutes of XT is recommended (pool running is best). Runners who did the preseason training could jog a very easy 20 minutes or cross-train.

Wednesday: Speed day. Standard warm-up, then 5 CDs and 4 Acgs (no sprinting). Then, run 6 x 400 (or .25 mi) about 2-3 seconds faster than current race pace for 2 Mile. Walk for 3 minutes between each. Then, use the standard warm-down.

Thursday: 4 HTs. Standard warm-up, then 3 Acgs. Then, run up a hill that is 60-90 yards long. Start each hill with 4-5 strides at a jog and gradually pick up the cadence of your feet. Shorten the stride as you ascend the hill, so that your leg motion feels smooth, with no straining. Glide slightly over the top of the hill and walk for 2 minutes. Then run gently down the hill with a short to medium stride, and "coast" out onto the flat for about 50 yards (practicing downhill running form). Don't race other runners, but fine-tune your own downhill technique as you stay under control. Don't let the stride get too long. Walk for 2 minutes and repeat the cycle. Afterwards, do a standard warm-down. It is OK to run this workout on the same type of terrain that will be run in the races, as long as the footing is stable. Those with unstable ankles should run hills on streets.

Friday: Off—you've earned a day of rest.

Saturday: Race or long run of 3 miles.

- Racers should not run at top speed or "all-out." Take it easy during the first mile. Pick up the pace a little in the second mile. On the third mile, pass a few runners. Many runners have found that a short walk break of 20-30 seconds, about every 4-5 minutes, helps them run faster than when running continuously. Don't sprint at the end, but you could gradually pick it up during the final 200 yards.

- If you're doing a long run, be sure to read the pace guidelines (three minutes per mile slower than race pace), and take the appropriate walk breaks, based upon pace per mile. You cannot run too slowly on the long run.

- If you are racing this weekend, jog a very slow 1 mile after the race—with lots of walk breaks.

Sunday: If there are no significant aches and pains, jog easily for 15-20 minutes or take the day off!

WEEK 4

Monday: Standard warm-up, 6 CDs, 5 Acgs (no sprinting). Then, run 1 mile at goal pace. Don't start too fast. Try to run each lap (or .25 mile) at the same pace. Walk for 5 minutes and run 2 x 400 (or .25 mi ea) about 2 seconds faster than race pace, but don't sprint! Walk half a lap between the 400s. Then do a standard warm-down. The track is still the best venue for this workout.

Tuesday: 20-30 minutes of XT is recommended (pool running is best). Runners who did the preseason training could jog a very easy 20-25 minutes or cross-train.

Wednesday: Speed day. Standard warm-up, then 5 CDs and 5 Acgs (no sprinting). Then, run 8 x 400 (or .25 mi). Run the first 2 x 400 about 6 seconds faster than current race pace for 2 Mile. Walk for 3 minutes between each. Run the last 6 x 400s, about 4 seconds faster than current race pace. Then, use the standard warm-down. This could be run on an accurately measured cross-country course, with stable footing (or the track).

Thursday: 4 HTs. Standard warm-up, then 3 Acgs. Then, run up a hill that is 70-100 yards long. Start each hill with 4-5 strides at a jog and gradually pick up the cadence of your feet. Shorten the stride as you ascend the hill, so that your leg motion feels smooth, with no straining. Glide slightly over the top of the hill and walk for 2 minutes. Then run gently down the hill with a short to medium stride, and "coast" out onto the flat for about 50 yards (practicing downhill running form). Don't race other runners, but fine-tune your own downhill technique as you stay under control. Don't let the stride get too long. Walk for 2 minutes and repeat the cycle. Afterwards, do a standard warm-down. It is OK to run this workout on the same type of terrain that will be run in the races, as long as the footing is stable. Those with unstable ankles should run hills on streets.

Friday: Off—you've earned a day of rest.

Saturday: Race or long run of 3.5 miles.

- Racers can start to run a little faster during the first 200 yards of the race (see chapter 13 on race strategies). Ease into a steady pace until the last half-mile of the race. During the last half-mile, try to pass one runner at a time. Don't sprint at the end, but you could gradually pick it up. No puking.

- If you're doing a long run (3.5 miles), be sure to read the pace guidelines (three minutes per mile slower than race pace), and take the appropriate walk breaks, based upon pace per mile. You cannot run too slowly on the long run.

- If you are racing this weekend, it will help to run very easily for 1.5 miles after the race, 3 min/mi slower than race pace.

Sunday: If there are no significant aches and pains, jog easily for 30 minutes or take the day off!

WEEK 5

Monday: Standard warm-up, 6 CDs, 5 Acgs (no sprinting). Then, a timed PTT (one mile). Your goal is to beat the best PTT so far. Pace yourself so that each lap (or .25 mile) is a little faster than the same unit on the best effort so far. Start to push yourself a little on the last lap without sprinting. The track is best for the PTT—to provide an accurate time comparison. Look at the tables in chapter 4 to see what your potential is currently in an ideal 5K on the track. This will allow you to continue focusing on a goal. Talk this over with the coach.

Tuesday: 20-30 minutes of XT is recommended (pool running is best). Runners who did the preseason training could jog a very easy 20 minutes or cross-train.

Wednesday: Speed day. Standard warm-up, then 5 CDs and 5 Acgs (no sprinting). Then, run 10 x 400 (or .25 mi). Run the first 2 x 400 about 8 seconds faster than current race pace for 2 Mile. Walk for 3 minutes between each. Run the last 8 x 400s, about 5 seconds faster than current race pace. Don't struggle, but stay smooth. Don't sprint at the end. Try to have consistent times on each. Then, use the standard warm-down. This could be run on an accurately measured cross-country course, with stable footing (or the track).

Thursday: 4 HTs. Standard warm-up, then 3 Acgs. Then, run up a hill that is 70-120 yards long. Start each hill with 4-5 strides at a jog and gradually pick up the cadence of your feet. Shorten the stride as you ascend the hill, so that your leg motion feels smooth, with no straining. Glide slightly over the top of the hill and walk for 2 minutes. Then run gently down the hill with a short to medium stride, and "coast" out onto the flat for about 50 yards (practicing downhill running form). Don't race other runners, but fine-tune your own downhill technique as you stay under control. Don't let the stride get too long. Walk for 2 minutes and repeat the cycle. Afterwards, do a standard warm-down. It is OK to run this workout on the same type of terrain that will be running in the races, as long as the footing is stable. Those with unstable ankles should run hills on streets.

Friday: Off—you've earned a day of rest.

Saturday: Race or long run of 4 miles.

- Racers should practice running a little faster during the first 200 yards of the race to get away from the mass of runners (see chapter 13 on race strategies). Ease into a steady pace until the last half-mile of the race. During the last half-mile, try to pass one runner at a time. Don't sprint at the end, but you could gradually pick it up. No puking.

- If you're doing a long run (4.5 miles), be sure to read the pace guidelines (three minutes per mile slower than race pace), and take the appropriate walk breaks, based upon pace per mile. You cannot run too slowly on the long run.

- If you are racing this weekend, run very easily for 2 miles after the race, 3 min/mi slower than race pace with lots of walk breaks. The long run of 4 miles could also be run on Sunday.

Sunday: If there are no significant aches and pains, jog easily for 30 minutes or take the day off!

WEEK 6

Monday: Standard warm-up, 6 CDs 6 Acgs (no sprinting). Then, run 1.5 miles at goal pace. It's OK to start a little faster than goal pace (for the first half lap) to get ready to run a little faster at the start of your cross-country races. Try to run each lap (or .25 mile) at the same pace. Walk for 5 minutes and run 2 x 400 (or .25 mi ea) about 2 seconds faster than race pace, but don't sprint! Walk half a lap between each. Then do a standard warm-down.

Tuesday: 20-30 minutes of XT is recommended (pool running is best). Runners who did the preseason training could jog a very easy 20 minutes or cross-train.

Wednesday: Speed day. Standard warm-up, then 5 CDs and 5 Acgs (no sprinting). Then, run 10-11 x 400 (or .25 mi). Run the first 2 x 400 about 8 seconds faster than current race pace for 2 Mile. Walk for 3 minutes between each. Run the remaining 400s, about

5 seconds faster than current race pace. Then, use the standard warm-down. This could be run on an accurately measured cross-country course, with stable footing (or the track).

Thursday: 4 HTs. Standard warm-up, then 3 Acgs. Then, run up a hill that is 70-150 yards long. Start each hill with 4-5 strides at a jog and gradually pick up the cadence of your feet. Shorten the stride as you ascend the hill, so that your leg motion feels smooth, with no straining. Glide slightly over the top of the hill and walk for 2 minutes. Then run gently down the hill with a short to medium stride, and "coast" out onto the flat for about 50 yards (practicing downhill running form). Don't race other runners, but fine-tune your own downhill technique as you stay under control. Don't let the stride get too long. Walk for 2 minutes and repeat the cycle. Afterwards, do a standard warm-down. It is OK to run this workout on the same type of terrain that will be run in the races, as long as the footing is stable. Those with unstable ankles should run hills on streets.

Friday: Off—you've earned a day of rest.

Saturday: Race or long run of 4.5 miles.

- Racers can run a little faster during the first 200 yards of the race (see chapter 13 on race strategies). Talk strategy to teammates and help one another. Ease into a steady pace until the last half-mile of the race. During the last mile, try to pass one runner at a time. Don't sprint at the end, but you could gradually pick it up. No puking.

- If you're doing a long run (4.5 miles), be sure to read the pace guidelines (three minutes per mile slower than race pace), and take the appropriate walk breaks, based upon pace per mile. You cannot run too slowly on the long run.

- If you are racing this weekend, run very easily for 2.5 miles after the race, 3 min/mi slower than race pace, with lots of walk breaks. The long run can be also run on Sunday.

Sunday: If there are no significant aches and pains, jog easily for 30 minutes or take the day off!

WEEK 7 GOAL RACE WEEK

Monday: Standard warm-up, 6 CDs, 6 Acgs (no sprinting). Run 1 mile. Talk strategy with teammates and start the workout. If possible, run on the race course or similar terrain. Run the first half-mile a little faster than goal pace, practicing race strategy. Try to run the second half-mile at goal pace. This is race practice and not competition—don't run too fast. Walk for 5 minutes. Then run a standard warm-down.

Tuesday: This should be a very easy day or a day off. XT is recommended (pool running is best for 20 minutes).

Wednesday: Speed day. This is the last speed workout before the first goal race, so save the effort for the race. Standard warm-up, then 5 CDs and 5 Acgs (no sprinting). Then, run 3 x 400 (or .25 mi) about 2-3 seconds faster than current race pace for 2 Mile. Walk for 3 minutes between each. Then, use the standard warm-down. This can be run on cross-country terrain.

Thursday: 2 HTs. Standard warm-up, then 4 Acgs. Don't push the effort on this workout—run for technique only. Run up each hill (60-100 yards long). Start each hill with 4-5 strides at a jog and gradually pick up the cadence of your feet. Shorten the stride as you ascend the hill, so that your leg motion feels smooth, with no straining. Glide slightly over the top of the hill and jog down gently. Afterwards, do a standard warm-down.

Friday: Off—rest for the race.

Saturday: Race!

- Racers should use the techniques that have worked well before, working with teammates when possible. Start just fast enough to get ahead of the bulk of the runners, but not so fast to leave the muscles exhausted during the last mile. Read chapter 13 on race strategies. During the second mile, try to pass one runner at a time to the finish. Don't save up for a final sprint—gradually pick it up during the last mile.

Sunday: If there are no significant aches and pains, jog easily for 30 minutes or take the day off!

- If you are running more races, alternate weeks 6 and 7

- If the season is over, congratulations. Enjoy running every other day or start training for another goal.

CHAPTER 10

2 MILE TRAINING PROGRAM (ALSO 3000-3200 METERS): VETERAN RUNNERS/TIME IMPROVEMENT

CD = Cadence Drill

Acg = Acceleration-Glider

XT = Cross-Training (water running is best)

HT = Hill Training (100-200 yds long)

PTT = Prediction Time Trial—1 mile

Standard warm-up: Walk 3 minutes, then 6 minutes of slow jogging, then running at a normal easy day running pace.

Standard warm-down: Jog for 4 minutes of running at a normal easy day running pace, then 10 minutes of very slow running.

Goal Pace: Confer with your coach about this. Most runners improve between 3-5% in a season.

 Only veterans who have done the preseason training should use this program. Otherwise, use the "Comeback" 5K program. Consult with your coach for adjustments.

WEEK 1

Monday: Standard warm-up, 4 cadence drills (CD), 2 acceleration gliders (Acg). Remember, no sprinting! Then, a timed Prediction Time Trial (PTT) (one mile). Run at an easy pace for the first half and speed up a little during the second half. Don't sprint or compete with the runners around you on this PTT. The goal today is just to record a time for the mile, under control. Coaches can use the PTT times to sort runners into groups. Standard warm-down afterward. The track is the best venue for this to limit the variables and develop pace judgment.

Tuesday: Those who have just restarted strenuous training should take the day off from running, or jog for 10-15 minutes. Cross-training (XT) is recommended (15 minutes of pool running is best). Runners who did the preseason training could jog a very easy 30 minutes or cross-train. Save the effort for Wednesday's workout.

Wednesday: Speed day. This is the first speed workout, so warm up well and don't run the first few repetitions too fast. Standard warm-up, then 4 CDs and 3 Acgs (no sprinting). Then, run 2 x 600 at current race pace for 2 Mile. The purpose of this workout is to be gentle in adapting to faster running. Walk for 3-4 minutes between each. Then, use the standard warm-down. During the first week, a track or a flat and stable surface is best for this workout.

Thursday: 2 Hills (HT). Standard warm-up, then 3 Acgs. Then, run up a hill that is 100-150 yards long. Start each hill with 4-5 strides at a jog and gradually pick up the cadence of your feet. Shorten the stride as you ascend the hill, so that your leg motion feels smooth, with no straining. Glide slightly over the top of the hill and walk down gently, then do the second hill. Afterwards, do a standard warm-down. It is OK to run this workout on the same type of terrain that will be used in the races, as long as the footing is stable. Those with unstable ankles should run on streets (or other stable terrain) for at least the first 2-3 weeks.

Friday: Off—you've earned a day of rest.

Saturday: Race or one mile time trial.

- Racers should not run even close to "all-out." Take it very easy during the first mile. Don't sprint at the end—try to hold your position. Only those who did the preseason training should be racing hard at this point in the season. Those who did not do the full preseason training could run an easy race this week.

Sunday: 3 miles (at least 3 min/mi slower than current 5K race pace). Be sure to insert walk breaks as noted in chapter 18. The long runs cannot be run too slowly, as running a bit too fast on long runs is a primary cause of injury.

WEEK 2

Monday: Standard warm-up, 5 CDs, 3 Acgs (no sprinting). Then, run a timed mile at goal pace. Don't start too fast. Try to run each lap (or .25 mile) at the same pace. Walk and jog for 5 minutes and run 2 x 400 meters at race pace or slightly faster. Then do a standard warm-down. This could be run on "cross-country terrain" as long as the footing is stable.

Tuesday: Run very easy for 2 miles, or do 20-30 minutes of XT. Running in the deep end of the pool can help one run smoother. It is fine to both run and cross- train.

Wednesday: Speed day (3 x 600 meter). This is the second speed workout and your body is still adjusting to fast running. Warm up well and don't run the first repetition too fast. Standard warm-up, then 4 CDs and 3 Acgs (no sprinting). Then, run the first 600 at current race pace for the 2 Mile. Walk and jog for 3 minutes and repeat. Run two more 600s, slightly faster than race pace. Then, use the standard warm- down. You can run on the same type of terrain as that used in races—as long as the surface is stable.

Thursday: 4 HTs. Standard warm-up, then 3 Acgs. Then, run up a hill that is 100-150 yards long. Start each hill with 4-5 strides at a jog and gradually pick up the cadence of your feet. Shorten the stride as you ascend the hill, so that your leg motion feels smooth, with no straining. Glide slightly over the top of the hill and walk for 2 minutes. Then run gently down the hill with a short to medium stride down and "coast" for about 50 yards on the flat (practicing a relaxed running form). Don't race other runners, and fine-tune your own downhill technique as you stay under control. Don't let the stride get too long. Walk for 2 minutes and repeat the cycle. Afterwards, do a standard warm-down. It is OK to run this workout on the same type of terrain that will be used in the races, as long as the footing is stable. Those with unstable ankles should run hills on streets.

Friday: Off—you've earned a day of rest.

Saturday: Race or long run of 3.5 miles.

- If this is the first race of the season, don't push into an "all-out" effort. Take it very easy during the first mile. If this is the second race of the season, you could run a little faster during the second half than in the first race. Don't sprint at the end, but you can gradually pick up the pace during the last half mile.

- If you're doing a long run (3.5 miles), be sure to read the pace guidelines, and take the appropriate walk breaks, based upon pace per mile. You cannot go too slowly on the long run.

- If you've races this weekend, run an additional 1.5 miles after the race, running 3 min/mi slower than race pace or slower with lots of walk breaks. You could also run the long run on Sunday—extra slowly.

Sunday: If there are no significant aches and pains, jog easily for 10-15 minutes or take the day off!

WEEK 3

Monday: Standard warm-up, 6 CDs, 4 Acgs (no sprinting). Then, a timed PTT (one mile). Your goal is to beat the time run in the first week. Pace yourself so that each lap (or .25 mile) is a little faster than the same unit on the first PTT. Don't sprint or compete with other runners on this PTT. Standard warm down. After the PTT, run 2 x 400 at goal race pace, jogging 200 meters between each. The track is the best venue for the PTT. Look at the tables in chapter 4 to see what your potential is currently in an ideal 2 miles on the track. Talk to your coach about your goal for the upcoming races. (Cross-country times tend to be slower than track times, for the same distance.)

Tuesday: 20 to 30 minutes of XT is recommended (pool running is best). Runners who did the preseason training could jog a very easy 20-30 minutes or cross-train.

Wednesday: Speed day. Standard warm-up, then 5 CDs and 4 Acgs (no sprinting). Then, run 4 x 600 about 4-6 seconds faster than current goal pace for 2 miles. Start running a little faster during the first 200 meters, then assume workout pace for the rest. Walk/jog slowly for 3 minutes between each. Then, use the standard warm-down. Cross-country race terrain is best for this workout as long as the surface is stable.

Thursday: 4 HTs. Standard warm-up, then 3 Acgs. Then, run up a hill that is 120-175 yards long. Start each hill with 4-5 strides at a jog and gradually pick up the cadence of your feet. Shorten the stride as you ascend the hill, so that your leg motion feels smooth, with no straining. Glide slightly over the top of the hill and walk for 2 minutes. Then run gently down the hill with a short to medium stride, and "coast" out onto the flat for about 50 yards (practicing downhill running form). Don't race other runners, but fine-tune your own downhill technique as you stay under control. Don't let the stride get too long. Walk for 2 minutes and repeat the cycle. Afterwards, do a standard warm-down. It is OK to run this workout on the same type of terrain that will be run in the races, as long as the footing is stable. Those with unstable ankles should run on streets.

Friday: Off—you've earned a day of rest.

Saturday: Race or long run of 4 miles.

- Racers should go out a little faster than they have been running for approximately 200 yards. Then work a good pace, but not too fast for the first mile. Pick up the pace a little in the second mile and pass a few runners. Don't sprint at the end, but you could gradually pick it up during the final 200 yards.

- If you're doing a long run, be sure to read the pace guidelines (three minutes per mile slower than race pace), and take the appropriate walk breaks, based upon pace per mile. You cannot run too slow on the long run.

- If you are racing this weekend, jog a very slow 2 miles after the race (3 min/mi slower than current race pace)—with lots of walk breaks. You can also run the long run on Sunday.

Sunday: If there are no significant aches and pains, jog easily for 15-20 minutes or take the day off!

WEEK 4

Monday: Standard warm-up, 6 CDs, 5 Acgs (no sprinting). Then, run 1.25 miles at goal pace. Don't start too fast. Try to run each lap (or .25 mile) at the same pace. Walk for 5 minutes and run 2 x 400 (or .25 mi ea) about 2 seconds faster than race pace, but don't sprint! Walk half a lap between the 400s. Then do a standard warm-down. Cross-country terrain is best for this workout—as long as the terrain is stable.

Tuesday: 20-30 minutes of XT is recommended (pool running is best). Runners who did the preseason training could jog a very easy 20-25 minutes or Cross-train. Save the effort for Wednesday's workout.

Wednesday: Speed day. Standard warm-up, then 5 CDs and 5 Acgs (no sprinting). Then, run 5 x 600. Run the first 2 x 600 about 8 seconds faster than goal race pace for 2 miles. During the first 200 meters of each 600, run a little faster than workout pace. Walk/jog for 3 minutes between each. Run the last 3 x 600s, about 5 seconds faster than goal race pace. Then, use the standard warm-down. The best venue is an accurately measured cross-country course, with stable footing (or the track).

Thursday: 4 HTs. Standard warm-up, then 3 Acgs. Then, run up a hill that is 125-200 yards long. Start each hill with 4-5 strides at a jog and gradually pick up the cadence of your feet. Shorten the stride as you ascend the hill, so that your leg motion feels smooth, with no straining. Glide slightly over the top of the hill and walk for 2 minutes. Then run gently down the hill with a short to medium stride, and "coast" out onto the flat for about 50 yards (practicing downhill running form). Don't race other runners, but fine-tune your own downhill technique as you stay under control. Don't let the stride get too long. Walk for 2 minutes and repeat the cycle. Afterwards, do a standard warm-down. It is OK to run this workout on the same type of terrain that will be run in the races, as long as the footing is stable. Those with unstable ankles should run hills on streets.

Friday: Off—you've earned a day of rest.

Saturday: Race or long run of 5 miles.

- Racers should run a little faster during the first 200 yards of the race (see chapter 13 on race strategies). Talk with teammates about strategy and help one another. After the first mile, try a strategy of catching up with the next group ahead, running with them for 100-200 yards, then passing for the next group or individual. Ease into a steady pace until the last half-mile of the race. During the last half-mile, try to pass one runner at a time. Don't sprint at the end, but you could gradually pick it up. No puking.

- If you're doing a long run (5 miles), be sure to read the pace guidelines (three minutes per mile slower than race pace), and take the appropriate walk breaks, based upon pace per mile. You cannot run too slowly on the long run.

- If you are racing this weekend, it will help to run very easily for 3 miles after the race, 3 min/mi slower than race pace with lots of walk breaks. You can also do the long run on Sunday—running extra slowly.

Sunday: If there are no significant aches and pains, jog easily for 30 minutes or take the day off!

WEEK 5

Monday: Standard warm-up, 6 CDs, 5 Acgs (no sprinting). Then, a timed PTT (one mile). Your goal is to beat the best PTT so far. Pace yourself so that each lap (or .25 mile) is a little faster than the same unit on the best effort so far. Start to push yourself a little on the last lap without sprinting. Walk for 5 minutes and do 3 x 400, 2-4 seconds faster than race pace, jogging 200 between each The track is best for the PTT—to provide an accurate time comparison. Look at the tables in chapter 4 to see what your potential is currently in an ideal 5K on the track. Talk to your coach about your goal for the upcoming races.

Tuesday: 20-30 minutes of XT is recommended (pool running is best). Runners who did the preseason training could jog a very easy 20 minutes or cross-train. Save your legs for Wednesday's workout.

Wednesday: Speed day. Standard warm-up, then 5 CDs and 5 Acgs (no sprinting). Then, run 6 x 600. Run the first 2 x 600 about 8 seconds faster than goal race pace for 2 miles. During the first 200 meters of each 600, run a little faster than workout pace to practice running fast at the beginning of the race. Walk/jog for 3 minutes between each. Run the last 4 x 600s, about 5 seconds faster than goal race pace. Then, use the standard warm-down. This could be run on an accurately measured cross-country course, with stable footing (or the track).

Thursday: 4-5 HTs. Standard warm-up, then 3 Acgs. Then, run up a hill that is 150-200 yards long. Start each hill with 4-5 strides at a jog and gradually pick up the cadence of your feet. Shorten the stride as you ascend the hill, so that your leg motion feels smooth, with no straining. Glide slightly over the top of the hill and walk for 2 minutes. Then run gently down the hill with a short to medium stride, and "coast" out onto the flat for about 50 yards (practicing downhill running form). Don't race other runners, but fine-tune your own downhill technique as you stay under control. Don't let the stride get too long. Walk for 2 minutes and repeat the cycle. Afterwards, do a standard warm-down. It is OK to run this workout on the same type of terrain that will be run in the races, as long as the footing is stable. Those with unstable ankles should run hills on streets.

Friday: Off—you've earned a day of rest.

Saturday: Race or long run of 6 miles.

- Racers should continue to run a little faster during the first 200 yards of the race (see chapter 13 on race strategies). Before the race, talk over strategy with your teammates. After the first mile, try a strategy of catching up with the next group ahead, running with them for 100-200 yards, then passing for the next group or individual. Ease into a steady pace until the last half mile of the race. During the last half mile, try to pass one runner at a time. Don't sprint at the end, but you could gradually pick it up. No puking.

- If you're doing a long run (6 miles), be sure to read the pace guidelines (three minutes per mile slower than race pace), and take the appropriate walk breaks, based upon pace per mile. You cannot run too slow on the long run.

- If you are racing this weekend, run very easily for 4 miles after the race, 3 min/mi slower than race pace (with lots of walk breaks), or run the long one on Sunday.

Sunday: If there are no significant aches and pains, jog easily for 30 minutes or take the day off!

WEEK 6

Monday: Standard warm-up, 6 CDs, 6 Acgs (no sprinting). Then, run 1.5 miles at goal pace. It's OK to start a little faster than goal pace to get ready to run a little faster at the start of your cross-country races. Try to run each lap (or .25 mile) at the same pace. Walk for 5 minutes and run 2 x 400 (or .25 mi ea) about 2-4 seconds faster than goal pace, but don't sprint! Walk half a lap between each. Then do a standard warm-down.

Tuesday: 20-30 minutes of XT is recommended (pool running is best). Runners who did the preseason training could jog a very easy 20 minutes or cross-train. Save your legs for Wednesday's workout.

Wednesday: Speed day. Standard warm-up, then 5 CDs and 5 Acgs (no sprinting). Then, run 7 x 600 meters. Run the first 2 x 600 about 8 seconds faster than goal race pace for 2 miles. During the first 200 meters of each 600, run a little faster than workout pace. Walk/jog for 3 minutes between each. Run the last 5 x 600s, about 5 seconds faster than goal race pace. Then, use the standard warm-down. The best venue is an accurately measured cross-country course, with stable footing (or the track).

Thursday: 4 HTs. Standard warm-up, then 3 Acgs. Then, run up a hill that is 100-150 yards long. Start each hill with 4-5 strides at a jog and gradually pick up the cadence of your feet. Shorten the stride as you ascend the hill, so that your leg motion feels smooth, with no straining. Glide slightly over the top of the hill and walk for 2 minutes. Then run gently down the hill with a short to medium stride, and "coast" out onto the flat for about 50 yards (practicing downhill running form). Don't race other runners, but fine-tune your own downhill technique as you stay under control. Don't let the stride get too long. Walk for 2 minutes and repeat the cycle. Afterwards, do a standard warm-down. It is OK to run this workout on the same type of terrain as in the races, as long as the footing is stable. Those with unstable ankles should run hills on streets.

Friday: Off—you've earned a day of rest.

Saturday: Race or long run of 6-7 miles.

- Racers can start to run a little faster during the first 200 yards of the race (see chapter 13 on race strategies). Talk over strategy with teammates and help one another. After the first mile, try a strategy of catching up with the next group ahead, running with them for 100-200 yards, then passing for the next group or individual. Ease into a steady pace until the last half mile of the race. During the last half mile, try to pass one runner at a time. Don't sprint at the end, but you could gradually pick it up. Smile!

- If you're doing a long run (6-7 miles), be sure to read the pace guidelines (three minutes per mile slower than race pace), and take the appropriate walk breaks, based upon pace per mile. You cannot run too slow on the long run.

- If you are racing this weekend, run very easily for 3-4 miles after the race, 3 min/mi slower than race pace with lots of walk breaks. The long run can also be run on Sunday.

Sunday: If there are no significant aches and pains, jog easily for 30 minutes or take the day off!

WEEK 7 GOAL RACE WEEK

Monday: Standard warm-up, 6 CDs, 6 Acgs (no sprinting). Then, run one mile for time. Talk strategy with teammates and start the workout. If possible, run on the race course or similar terrain. Run the first half mile a little faster than goal pace, practicing race strategy. Try to run the second half mile at goal pace. This is race practice and not competition—don't run too fast. Walk for 5 minutes and run 2 x 400 (or .25 mi ea) at about race pace. Walk about 200 meters between each. Then do a standard warm-down.

Tuesday: This should be a very easy day or a day off. XT is recommended (pool running is best for 20 minutes).

Wednesday: Speed day. This is the last speed workout before the first goal race, so save the effort for the race. Standard warm-up, then 5 CDs and 5 Acgs (no sprinting). Then, run 3 x 400 (or .25 mi) about 2-3 seconds faster than current race pace for 2 miles. Walk for 3 minutes between each. Then, use the standard warm-down. This can be run on cross-country terrain.

Thursday: 2 HTs. Standard warm-up, then 4 Acgs. Don't push the pace on these hills, just work on form and technique. Run up each hill (100-150 yards long). Start each hill with 4-5 strides at a jog and gradually pick up the cadence of your feet. Shorten the stride as you ascend the hill, so that your leg motion feels smooth, with no straining. Glide slightly over the top of the hill and jog down gently. Afterwards, do a standard warm-down.

Friday: Off—rest for the race.

Saturday: Race!

- Racers should use the techniques that have worked well before, working with teammates when possible. Start just fast enough to get ahead of the bulk of the runners, but not so fast to leave the muscles exhausted durinq the last mile. Read chapter 13 on race strategies. During the second mile, try to pass one runner at a time to the finish. Don't save up for a final sprint—gradually pick it up during the last mile.

Sunday: If there are no significant aches and pains, jog easily for 30 minutes or take the day off!

- If you are running more races, alternate weeks 6 and 7.

- If the season is over, congratulations. Enjoy running every other day or start training for another goal.

CHAPTER 11

1 MILE/1500 METERS:
BEGINNER OR COMEBACK RUNNERS

CD = Cadence Drill

Acg = Acceleration-Glider

XT = Cross-Training (water running is best)

HT = Hill Training (40-100 yds long)

PTT = Prediction Time Trial—800 meters

Standard warm-up: Walk 3 minutes, then 6 minutes of run 1 minute/walk 20 seconds, then jog for 4 minutes slowly.

Standard warm-down: Jog for 4 minutes very slowly, then 6 minutes run 1 minute/walk for 20 seconds, then walk for 5 minutes.

Goal Pace: Athletes should talk to their coach about this. Most runners improve between 3-5% in a season.

WEEK 1—PRIME MISSION: STAY INJURY-FREE

Monday: Standard warm-up, 4 cadence drills (CD), 2 acceleration-gliders (Acg). Remember, no sprinting! Then, a timed Prediction Time Trial (PTT) (800 meters). Run at an easy pace for the first 400 (.25 mile) and speed up a little during the second 400. Don't sprint or compete with the runners around you on this PTT. The goal today is just to record a time for the 800, under control without hurting. Coaches can use the PTT times to sort runners into groups. Standard warm-down afterward. The track is the best venue for this, to limit the variables and develop pace judgment.

Tuesday: Those who are just starting should take the day off from running. Cross-training (XT) is recommended (10-15 minutes of pool running is best). Runners who did the preseason training could jog a very easy 10 minutes or cross-train.

Wednesday: Speed day. This is the first speed workout so don't run too fast. Standard warm-up, then 4 CDs and 3 Acgs (no sprinting). Then, run 2 x 400 (or .25 mi) at current race pace for 1 Mile. The strategy of this workout is to be gentle in adapting to faster running. Walk for 3 minutes between each. Then, use the standard warm-down. A track is best for this workout to learn pace judgment.

Thursday: 2 Hills (HT). Standard warm-up, then 3 Acgs. Then, run up a hill that is 40-60 yards long. Start each hill with 4-5 strides at a jog and gradually pick up the cadence of your feet. Shorten the stride as you ascend the hill, so that your leg motion feels smooth, with no straining. Glide slightly over the top of the hill and walk down gently, then do the second hill. Afterwards, do a standard warm-down. It is OK to run this workout on the same type of terrain that will be used in the races, as long as the footing is stable. Those with unstable ankles should run hills on streets for at least the first 2-3 weeks.

Friday: Off—you've earned a day of rest.

Saturday: Race or long run of 1.5 miles.

- Racers should not run even close to "all-out." Take it very easy during the first half. Many runners have found that a short walk break of 20-30 seconds, about every 2-3 minutes, helps them run faster than when running continuously. Don't sprint at the end—try to hold your position. Only those who did the preseason training should be racing hard at this point in the season. If this was your first week of training it is best to do the long run instead.

- If you're doing a long run (1.5 miles), be sure to read the pace guidelines (3 min/mi slower than race pace), and take the appropriate walk breaks, based upon pace per mile. Those who did not do the preseason training should use a run-walk-run of run 1 minute/walk 1 minute.

Sunday: Take the day off!

WEEK 2

Monday: Standard warm-up, 5 CDs, 3 Acgs (no sprinting). Then, run a timed 400 meters (.25 mile) at goal pace. Don't start too fast. Try to run each lap (or .25 mile) at the same pace. Walk for 5 minutes and run a 400 (or .25 mi) at race pace. Then do a standard warm-down. The track is a great venue for this workout. Don't run at so hard that you experience pain.

Tuesday: Those who are just starting should take the day off from running. Fifteen to twenty minutes of XT is recommended (pool running is best). Runners who did the preseason training could jog a very easy 10 minutes or cross-train.

Wednesday: Speed day. Your body is still trying to adapt to faster running, so don't run too fast. Standard warm-up, then 4 CDs and 3 Acgs (no sprinting). Then, run 3 x 400 (or .25 mi) at current race pace for 1 mile. The purpose of this workout is to be gentle in adapting to faster running. Walk for 3 minutes between each. Then, use the standard warm-down. The track is also suggested for this workout—to learn pace judgment.

Thursday: 3 HTs. Standard warm-up, then 3 Acgs. Then, run up a hill that is 40-60 yards long. Start each hill with 4-5 strides at a jog and gradually pick up the cadence of your feet. Shorten the stride as you ascend the hill, so that your leg motion feels smooth, with no straining. Glide slightly over the top of the hill and walk for 2 minutes. Then run gently down the hill with a short to medium stride and "coast" for about 50 yards on the flat (practicing a relaxed running form). Don't race other runners, and fine- tune your own downhill technique as you stay under control. Don't let the stride get too long. Walk for 2 minutes and repeat the cycle. Afterwards, do a standard warm-down. It is OK to run this workout on the same type of terrain that will be used in the races, as long as the footing is stable. Those with unstable ankles should run hills on streets.

Friday: Off—you've earned a day of rest.

Saturday: Race or long run of 1.75 miles.

- If this is the first race of the season, don't run "all-out." Take it very easy during the first half. If this is the second race of the season, you could run a little faster during the second half than you ran in the first race. Many runners have found that a short walk break of 20-30 seconds, about every 2-3 minutes, helps them run faster than when running continuously—with more strength at the end. Don't sprint at the end, but you can gradually pick up the pace during the last mile.

- If you're doing a long run (1.75 miles), be sure to read the pace guidelines, and take the appropriate walk breaks, based upon pace per mile. You cannot go too slowly on the long run.

- If you raced on Saturday, you can either do the slow long run on Sunday or run a very slow .75 run after the race.

Sunday: If there are no significant aches and pains, jog easily for 10-15 minutes or take the day off!

WEEK 3

Monday: Standard warm-up, 6 CDs, 4 Acgs (no sprinting). Then, a timed PTT (800 meters). Your goal is to beat the time run in the first week. Pace yourself so that each lap (or .25 mile) is a little faster than the same unit on the first PTT. Don't sprint or compete with other runners on this PTT. Standard warm-down. The track is the best venue for the PTT. Look at the tables in chapter 4 to note your current potential in an ideal 1 Mile on the track. This will allow you to start focusing on a goal. (Cross-country times tend to be slower than track times, for the same distance.)

Tuesday: 20 to 30 minutes of XT is recommended (pool running is best). Runners who did the preseason training could jog a very easy 15 minutes or cross-train.

Wednesday: Speed day. Standard warm-up, then 5 CDs and 4 Acgs (no sprinting). Then, run 4 x 400 (or .25 mi) about 1-2 seconds faster than current race pace for 1 Mile. Walk for 3 minutes between each. Then, use the standard warm-down.

Thursday: 4 HTs. Standard warm-up, then 3 Acgs. Then, run up a hill that is 40-75 yards long. Start each hill with 4-5 strides at a jog and gradually pick up the cadence of your feet. Shorten the stride as you ascend the hill, so that your leg motion feels smooth, with no straining. Glide slightly over the top of the hill and walk for 2 minutes. Then run gently down the hills with a short to medium stride, and "coast" out onto the flat for about 50 yards (practicing downhill running form). Don't race other runners, but fine-tune your own downhill technique as you stay under control. Don't let the stride get too long. Walk for 2 minutes and repeat the cycle. Afterwards, do a standard warm-down. It is OK to run this workout on the same type of terrain that you'll be running in the races, as long as the footing is stable. Those with unstable ankles should run hills on streets.

Friday: Off—you've earned a day of rest.

Saturday: Race or long run of 2 miles.

- Racers should not run at top speed or "all-out". Take it easy during the first half. Pick up the pace a little in the second half. During the final 300 yards, pass a few runners. Use walk breaks as needed. Don't sprint at the end.

- If you're doing a long run, be sure to read the pace guidelines (three minutes per mile slower than race pace), and take the appropriate walk breaks, based upon pace per mile. You cannot run too slow on the long run.

- If you raced this weekend, you could run the long one on Sunday or jog a very slow 1 mile after the race—with lots of walk breaks.

Sunday: If there are no significant aches and pains, jog easily for 15-20 minutes or take the day off!

WEEK 4

Monday: Standard warm-up, 6 CDs, 5 Acgs (no sprinting). Then, run 800 meters (.5 mile) at goal pace. Don't start too fast. Try to run each lap (or .25 mile) at the same pace. Walk for 5 minutes and run 1 x 400 (or .25 mi ea) about 2 seconds faster than race pace, but don't sprint! Then do a standard warm-down. The track is still the best venue for this workout.

Tuesday: 20-30 minutes of XT is recommended (pool running is best). Runners who did the preseason training could jog a very easy 20-25 minutes or cross-train.

Wednesday: Speed day. Standard warm-up, then 5 CDs and 5 Acgs (no sprinting). Then, run 6 x 400 (or .25 mi). Run the first 2 x 400 about 5 seconds faster than current race pace for 2 miles. Walk for 3 minutes between each. Run the last 4 x 400s, about 3 seconds faster than current race pace. Then, use the standard warm-down. This could be run on an accurately measured cross- country course, with stable footing (or the track).

Thursday: 4 HTs. Standard warm-up, then 3 Acgs. Then, run up a hill that is 75-100 yards long. Start each hill with 4-5 strides at a jog and gradually pick up the cadence of your feet. Shorten the stride as you ascend the hill, so that your leg motion feels smooth, with no straining. Glide slightly over the top of the hill and walk for 2 minutes. Then run gently down the hill with a short to medium stride, and "coast" out onto the flat for about 50 yards (practicing downhill running form). Don't race other runners, but fine-tune your own downhill technique as you stay under control. Don't let the stride get too long. Walk for 2 minutes and repeat the cycle. Afterwards, do a standard warm-down. It is OK to run this workout on the same type of terrain that will be run in the races, as long as the footing is stable. Those with unstable ankles should run hills on streets.

Friday: Off—you've earned a day of rest.

Saturday: Race or long run of 2.25 miles.

- Racers can start to run a little faster during the first 200 yards of the race (see chapter 13 on race strategies). Ease into a steady pace until the last half-mile of the race. During the last half-mile, try to pass one runner at a time. Don't sprint at the end, but you could gradually pick it up. No puking.

- If you're doing a long run (2.25 miles), be sure to read the pace guidelines (three minutes per mile slower than race pace), and take the appropriate walk breaks, based upon pace per mile. You cannot run too slowly on the long run.

- If you raced this weekend, run very easily for 1.5 miles after the race, 3 min/mi slower than race pace—with as many walk breaks as you wish.

Sunday: If there are no significant aches and pains, jog easily for 30 minutes or take the day off!

WEEK 5

Monday: Standard warm-up, 6 CDs, 5 Acgs (no sprinting). Then, a timed PTT (800 meters or half a mile). Your goal is to beat the best PTT so far. Pace yourself so that each lap (or .25 mile) is a little faster than the same unit during your best effort so far. Start to push yourself a little on the last lap without sprinting. The track is best for the PTT—to provide an accurate time comparison. Look at the tables in chapter 4 to see what your current potential is for an ideal mile race on the track, currently. This will allow you to continue focusing on a goal. Talk this over with the coach.

Tuesday: 20-30 minutes of XT is recommended (pool running is best). Runners who did the preseason training could jog a very easy 20 minutes or cross-train. Save your legs for Wednesday's workout.

Wednesday: Speed day. Standard warm-up, then 5 CDs and 5 Acgs (no sprinting). Then, run 8 x 400 (or .25 mi). Run the first 2 x 400 about 5 seconds faster than current race pace for 2 Mile. Walk for 3 minutes between each. Run the last 6 x 400s, about 3 seconds faster than current race pace. Don't struggle, but stay smooth. Don't sprint at the end. Try to have consistent times on each. Then, use the standard warm-down. This could be run on an accurately measured cross-country course, with stable footing (or the track).

Thursday: 4 HTs. Standard warm-up, then 3 Acgs. Then, run up a hill that is 75-100 yards long. Start each hill with 4-5 strides at a jog and gradually pick up the cadence of your feet. Shorten the stride as you ascend the hill, so that your leg motion feels smooth, with no straining. Glide slightly over the top of the hill and walk for 2 minutes. Then run gently down the hill with a short to medium stride, and "coast" out onto the flat for about 50 yards (practicing downhill running form). Don't race other runners, but fine-tune your own downhill technique as you stay under control. Don't let the stride get too long. Walk for 2 minutes and repeat the cycle. Afterwards, do a standard warm-down. It is OK to run this workout on the same type of terrain that will be running in the races, as long as the footing is stable. Those with unstable ankles should run hills on streets.

Friday: Off—you've earned a day of rest.

Saturday: Race or long run of 2.5 miles.

- Racers should practice running a little faster during the first 200 yards of the race to get away from the mass of the crowd (see chapter 13 on race strategies). Ease into a steady pace until the last half-mile of the race. During the last half-mile, try to pass one runner at a time. Don't sprint at the end, but you could gradually pick it up. No puking.

- If you're doing a long run (2.5 miles), be sure to read the pace guidelines (three minutes per mile slower than race pace), and take the appropriate walk breaks, based upon pace per mile. You cannot run too slowly on the long run.

- If you are racing this weekend, run very easily for 1.5 miles after the race, 3 min/mi slower than race pace, taking walk breaks as you wish. The long run of 2.5 miles could also be run on Sunday.

Sunday: If there are no significant aches and pains, jog easily for 30 minutes or take the day off!

WEEK 6

Monday: Standard warm-up, 6 CDs, 6 Acgs (no sprinting). Then, run .75 miles at goal pace. Try to run each lap (or .25 mile) at the same pace. Walk for 5 minutes and run 2 x 400 (or .25 mi ea) about 2 seconds faster than race pace, but don't sprint! Walk half a lap between each. Then do a standard warm-down.

Tuesday: 20-30 minutes of XT is recommended (pool running is best). Runners who did the preseason training could jog a very easy 20 minutes or cross-train. It is also OK to take the day off in preparation for the Wednesday workout.

Wednesday: Speed day. Standard warm-up, then 5 CDs and 5 Acgs (no sprinting). Then, run 9 x 400 (or .25 mi). Run the first 2 x 400 about 5 seconds faster than current race pace for 2 Mile. Walk for 3 minutes between each. Run the remaining 400s, about 3 seconds faster than current race pace. Then, use the standard warm-down. This could be run on an accurately measured cross-country course, with stable footing (or the track).

Thursday: 4 HTs. Standard warm-up, then 3 Acgs. Then, run up a hill that is 75-100 yards long. Start each hill with 4-5 strides at a jog and gradually pick up the cadence of your feet. Shorten the stride as you ascend the hill, so that your leg motion feels smooth, with no straining. Glide slightly over the top of the hill and walk for 2 minutes. Then run gently down the hill with a short to medium stride, and "coast" out onto the flat for about 50 yards (practicing downhill running form). Don't race other runners, but fine-tune your own downhill technique as you stay under control. Don't let the stride get too long. Walk for 2 minutes and repeat the cycle. Afterwards, do a standard warm-down. It is OK to run this workout on the same type of terrain that will be run in the races, as long as the footing is stable. Those with unstable ankles should run hills on streets.

Friday: Off—you've earned a day of rest.

Saturday: Race or long run of 2.75-3 miles.

- Racers can run a little faster during the first 200 yards of the race (see chapter 13 on race strategies). Talk over strategy with teammates. Ease into a steady pace until the last quarter mile of the race. During this finish, try to pass one runner at a time. Don't sprint at the end, but you could gradually pick it up. No puking.

- If you're doing a long run (2.75-3 miles), be sure to read the pace guidelines (three minutes per mile slower than race pace), and take the appropriate walk breaks, based upon pace per mile. You cannot run too slowly on the long run.

- If you are racing this weekend, run very easily for 1.75-2 miles after the race, 3 min/ mi slower than race pace. The long run can be also run on Sunday.

Sunday: If there are no significant aches and pains, jog easily for 30 minutes or take the day off!

WEEK 7 GOAL RACE WEEK

Monday: Standard warm-up, 6 CDs, 6 Acgs (no sprinting). Run 800 meters (half a mile). Talk strategy with teammates and start the workout. If possible, run on the race course or similar terrain. Run the first quarter mile (400 meters) a little faster than goal pace, practicing race strategy. Try to run the second half-mile at goal pace. This is race practice and not competition—don't run too fast. Walk for 5 minutes. Then run a standard warm-down.

Tuesday: This should be a very easy day or a day off. XT is recommended (pool running is best for 20 minutes).

Wednesday: Speed day. This is the last speed workout before the first goal race, so save the effort for the race. Standard warm-up, then 5 CDs and 5 Acgs (no sprinting). Then, run 2 x 400 (or .25 mi) about 2-3 seconds faster than current race pace for 1 Mile. Walk for 3 minutes between each. Then, use the standard warm-down. This can be run on cross-country terrain.

Thursday: 2 HTs. Standard warm-up, then 4 Acgs. Don't push the effort on this workout—run for technique only. Run up each hill (60-100 yards long). Start each hill with 4-5 strides at a jog and gradually pick up the cadence of your feet. Shorten the stride as you ascend the hill, so that your leg motion feels smooth, with no straining. Glide slightly over the top of the hill and jog down gently. Afterwards, do a standard warm-down.

Friday: Off—rest for the race.

Saturday: Race!

- Racers should use the techniques that have worked well before, working with teammates when possible. Start just fast enough to get ahead of the bulk of the runners, but not so fast to leave the muscles exhausted during the last quarter mile. Read chapter 13 on race strategies. During the second half, try to pass one runner at a time to the finish. Don't save up for a final sprint—gradually pick it up during the last half mile.

Sunday: If there are no significant aches and pains, jog easily for 30 minutes or take the day off!

- If you are running more races, alternate weeks 6 and 7

- If the season is over, congratulations. Enjoy running every other day or start training for another goal.

D 1656

2E 1857

2L 2904

2G 2205

CHAPTER 12

1 MILE TRAINING PROGRAM (ALSO 1500 METERS): VETERAN RUNNERS/TIME IMPROVEMENT

CD = Cadence Drill

Acg = Acceleration-Glider

XT = Cross-Training (water running is best)

HT = Hill Training (100-200 yds long)

PTT = Prediction Time Trial—800 meter

Standard warm-up: Walk 3 minutes, then 6 minutes of slow jogging, then running at a normal easy day running pace.

Standard warm-down: Jog for 4 minutes of running at a normal easy day running pace, then 10 minutes of very slow running.

Goal Pace: Confer with your coach about this. Most runners improve between 3-5% in a season.

NOTE: Only veterans who have done the preseason training should use this program. Otherwise, use the "Comeback" program (chapter 11).

WEEK 1

Monday: Standard warm-up, 4 cadence drills (CD), 2 acceleration-gliders (Acg). Remember, no sprinting! Then, a timed Prediction Time Trial (PTT) (one mile). Run at an easy pace for the first half and speed up a little during the second half. Don't sprint or compete with the runners around you on this PTT. The goal today is just to record a time for the mile, under control. Coaches can use the PTT times to sort runners into groups. Standard warm-down afterward. The track is the best venue for this, to limit the variables and develop pace judgment.

Tuesday: Those who have recently returned to strenuous training should take the day off from running, or jog for 10-15 minutes. Cross-training (XT) is recommended (15 minutes of pool running is best). Runners who did the preseason training could jog a very easy 30 minutes or cross-train.

Wednesday: Speed day. This is the first speed workout so warm up well and don't run the first few repetitions too fast. Standard warm-up, then 4 CDs and 3 Acgs (no sprinting). Then, run 3 x 400 at current race pace for 1 Mile, or a little slower. The purpose of this workout is to be gentle in adapting to faster running. Walk for 3-4 minutes between each. Then, use the standard warm-down. During the first week, a track or a flat and stable surface is best for this workout.

Thursday: 2 Hills (HT). Standard warm-up, then 3 Acgs. Then, run up a hill that is 100 yards long. Start each hill with 4-5 strides at a jog and gradually pick up the cadence of your feet. Shorten the stride as you ascend the hill, so that your leg motion feels smooth, with no straining. Glide slightly over the top of the hill and walk down gently, then do the second hill. Afterwards, do a standard warm-down. It is OK to run this workout on the same type of terrain that will be used in the races, as long as the footing is stable. Those with unstable ankles should run on streets (or other stable terrain) for at least the first 2-3 weeks.

Friday: Off—you've earned a day of rest.

Saturday: Race or 3 mile long run

- Racers should not run even close to "all-out". Take it very easy during the first mile. Don't sprint at the end—try to hold your position. Only those who did the preseason training should be racing hard at this point in the season. Those who did not do the full preseason training could run an easy race this week.

Sunday: 3 miles (at least 3 min/mi slower than current 1 mile race pace). Be sure to insert walk breaks as noted in chapter 18. The long runs cannot be run too slowly. In contrast, running a bit too fast on long runs is a primary cause of injury.

WEEK 2

Monday: Standard warm-up, 5 CDs, 3 Acgs (no sprinting). Then, run a timed 600 meter at goal pace. Don't start too fast. Try to run each 200 meter at the same pace. Walk and jog for 5 minutes and run 2 x 400 meters at race pace or slightly faster (with 3 minutes of rest between each). Then do a standard warm-down. The best venue is the track for this.

Tuesday: Run very easy for 2 miles, or do 20-30 minutes of XT. Running in the deep end of the pool can help one run smoother. It is fine to both run and cross-train.

Wednesday: Speed day (4 x 400 meter). This is the second speed workout and your body is still adjusting to fast running. Warm up well and don't run the first repetition too fast. Standard warm-up, then 4 CDs and 3 Acgs (no sprinting). Then, run the first and second 400 at current race pace for the Mile or slightly slower. Walk and jog for 3 minutes and repeat. Run two more 400s, slightly faster than race pace. Then, use the standard warm-down. You can run on the same type of terrain as that used in races—as long as the surface is stable.

Thursday: 4 HTs. Standard warm-up, then 3 Acgs. Then, run up a hill that is 100-150 yards long. Start each hill with 4-5 strides at a jog and gradually pick up the cadence of your feet. Shorten the stride as you ascend the hill, so that your leg motion feels smooth, with no straining. Glide slightly over the top of the hill and walk for 2 minutes. Then run gently down the hill with a short to medium stride down and "coast" for about 50 yards on the flat (practicing a relaxed running form). Don't race other runners, and fine-tune your own downhill technique as you stay under control. Don't let the stride get too long. Walk for 2 minutes and repeat the cycle. Afterwards, do a standard warm-down. It is OK to run this workout on the same type of terrain that will be used in the races, as long as the footing is stable. Those with unstable ankles should run hills on streets.

Friday: Off—you've earned a day of rest.

Saturday: Race or long run of 3.5 miles.

- If this is the first race of the season, don't push into an "all-out" effort. Take it very easy during the first half-mile. If this is the second race of the season, you could run a little faster during the second half than in the first race. Don't sprint at the end, but you can gradually pick up the pace during the last mile.

- If you're doing a long run (3.5 miles), be sure to read the pace guidelines, and take the appropriate walk breaks, based upon pace per mile. You cannot go too slowly on the long run.

- If you raced this weekend, run an additional 2.5 miles after the race, running 3 min/mi slower than race pace—or slower and taking as many walk breaks as you wish. You could also run the long run on Sunday—extra slowly.

Sunday: If there are no significant aches and pains, jog easily for 10-15 minutes or take the day off!

WEEK 3

Monday: Standard warm-up, 6 CDs, 4 Acgs (no sprinting). Then, a timed PTT (800 meters). Your goal is to beat the time run in the first week. Pace yourself so that each lap (or .25 mile) is a little faster than the same unit on the first PTT. Don't sprint or compete with other runners on this PTT. After the PTT, run 2 x 400 at goal race pace, jogging 200 meters between each. The track is the best venue for the PTT. Do a standard warm-down. Look at the tables in chapter 4 to see what your potential is currently in an ideal 2 miles on the track. Talk to your coach about your goal for the upcoming races. (Cross-country times tend to be slower than track times, for the same distance.)

Tuesday: 20 to 30 minutes of XT is recommended (pool running is best). Runners who did the preseason training could jog a very easy 20 minutes or cross-train.

Wednesday: Speed day. Standard warm-up, then 5 CDs and 4 Acgs (no sprinting). Then, run 5 x 400 about 2-3 seconds faster than current goal pace for 1 mile. Start running a little faster during the first 100 meters, then assuming workout pace for the rest. Walk/jog slowly for 3 minutes between each. Then, use the standard warm-down. Cross-country race terrain is best for this workout as long as the surface is stable.

Thursday: 4 HTs. Standard warm-up, then 3 Acgs. Then, run up a hill that is 100-175 yards long. Start each hill with 4-5 strides at a jog and gradually pick up the cadence of your feet. Shorten the stride as you ascend the hill, so that your leg motion feels smooth, with no straining. Glide slightly over the top of the hill and walk for 2 minutes. Then run gently down the hill with a short to medium stride, and "coast" out onto the flat for about 50 yards (practicing downhill running form). Don't race other runners, but fine-tune your own downhill technique as you stay under control. Don't let the stride get too long. Walk for 2 minutes and repeat the cycle. Afterwards, do a standard warm-down. It is OK to run this workout on the same type of terrain that will be run in the races, as long as the footing is stable. Those with unstable ankles should run on streets.

Friday: Off—you've earned a day of rest.

Saturday: Race or long run of 4 miles.

- Racers should go out a little faster than they have been running for 200 yards. Then settle into a pace that is a little slower than goal pace. Pick up the pace a little in the second half and pass a few runners. Don't sprint at the end, but you could gradually pick it up during the final 200 yards.

- If you're doing a long run, be sure to read the pace guidelines (three minutes per mile slower than race pace), and take the appropriate walk breaks, based upon pace per mile. You cannot run too slow on the long run.

- If you are racing this weekend, jog a very slow 3 miles after the race (3 min/mi slower than current race pace)—with lots of walk breaks.

Sunday: If there are no significant aches and pains, jog easily for 15-20 minutes or take the day off!

WEEK 4

Monday: Standard warm-up, 6 CDs, 5 Acgs (no sprinting). Then, run 1000 meters at goal pace. Don't start too fast. Try to run each lap (or .25 mile) at the same pace. Walk for 5 minutes and run 2 x 400 (or .25 mi ea) about 2 seconds faster than race pace, but don't sprint! Walk half a lap between the 400s. Then do a standard warm-down. Cross-country terrain is best for this workout—as long as the terrain is stable.

Tuesday: 20-30 minutes of XT is recommended (pool running is best). Runners who did the preseason training could jog a very easy 20-25 minutes or cross-train.

Wednesday: Speed day. Standard warm-up, then 5 CDs and 5 Acgs (no sprinting). Then, run 6 x 400. Run the first 2 x 400 about 6 seconds faster than goal race pace for 2 miles. During the first 200 meters of each 600, run a little faster than workout pace. Jog for 3 minutes between each. Run the last 4 x 400s, about 3 seconds faster than current race pace. Then, use the standard warm-down. The best venue is an accurately measured cross-country course, with stable footing (or the track).

Thursday: 4 HTs. Standard warm-up, then 3 Acgs. Then, run up a hill that is 125-200 yards long. Start each hill with 4-5 strides at a jog and gradually pick up the cadence of your feet. Shorten the stride as you ascend the hill, so that your leg motion feels smooth, with no straining. Glide slightly over the top of the hill and walk for 2 minutes. Then run gently down the hill with a short to medium stride, and "coast" out onto the flat for about 50 yards (practicing downhill running form). Don't race other runners, but fine-tune your own downhill technique as you stay under control. Don't let the stride get too long. Walk for 2 minutes and repeat the cycle. Afterwards, do a standard warm-down. It is OK to run this workout on the same type of terrain that will be run in the races, as long as the footing is stable. Those with unstable ankles should run hills on streets.

Friday: Off—you've earned a day of rest.

Saturday: Race or long run of 4.5 miles.

- Racers can start to run a little faster during the first 200 yards of the race (see chapter 13 for race strategies). After the first half, try a strategy of catching up with the next group ahead, running with them for 100-200 yards, then passing for the next group or individual. Ease into a steady pace until the last 200 yards of the race. During the last half-mile, try to pass one runner at a time. Don't sprint at the end, but you could gradually pick it up. No puking.

- If you're doing a long run (4.5 miles), be sure to read the pace guidelines (three minutes per mile slower than race pace), and take the appropriate walk breaks, based upon pace per mile. You cannot run too slow on the long run.

- If you are racing this weekend, it will help to run very easily for 3 miles after the race, 3 min/mi slower than race pace. You can also do the long run on Sunday— running extra slowly.

Sunday: If there are no significant aches and pains, jog easily for 20 minutes or take the day off!

WEEK 5

Monday: Standard warm-up, 6 CDs, 5 Acgs (no sprinting). Then, a timed PTT (800 meters). Your goal is to beat the best PTT so far. Pace yourself so that each lap (or .25 mile) is a little faster than the same unit on the best effort so far. Start to push yourself a little on the last lap without sprinting. Walk for 5 minutes and do 2 x 400, 2 seconds faster than race pace, jogging 200 between each The track is best for the PTT—to provide an accurate time comparison. Look at the tables in chapter 4 to see what your potential is currently on the track. Talk to your coach about your goal for the upcoming races.

Tuesday: 20-30 minutes of XT is recommended (pool running is best). Runners who did the preseason training could jog easily for 20 minutes or cross-train.

Wednesday: Speed day. Standard warm-up, then 5 CDs and 5 Acgs (no sprinting). Then, run 6 x 400. Run the first 2 x 600 about 6 seconds faster than goal race pace for 2 miles. During the first 200 meters of each 400, run a little faster than workout pace—to practice running fast at the beginning your race. Jog for 2 minutes between each. Run the last 4 x 600s, about 4 seconds faster than current race pace. Then, use the standard warm-down. This could be run on an accurately measured cross- country course, with stable footing (or the track).

Thursday: 4-5 HTs. Standard warm-up, then 3 Acgs. Then, run up a hill that is 125-200 yards long. Start each hill with 4-5 strides at a jog and gradually pick up the cadence of your feet. Shorten the stride as you ascend the hill, so that your leg motion feels smooth, with no straining. Glide slightly over the top of the hill and walk for 2 minutes. Then run gently down the hill with a short to medium stride, and "coast" out onto the flat for about 50 yards (practicing downhill running form). Don't race other runners, but fine-tune your own downhill technique as you stay under control. Don't let the stride get too long. Walk for 2 minutes and repeat the cycle. Afterwards, do a standard warm-down. It is OK to run this workout on the same type of terrain that will be run in the races, as long as the footing is stable. Those with unstable ankles should run hills on streets.

Friday: Off—you've earned a day of rest.

Saturday: Race or long run of 5 miles.

- Racers can run a little faster during the first 200 yards of the race (see chapter 13 on race strategies). After the first half, try a strategy of catching up with the next group ahead, running with them for 100-200 yards, then passing for the next group or individual. Ease into a steady pace until the last 200 yards. Try to pass one runner at a time. Don't sprint at the end, but you could gradually pick it up. No puking.

- If you're doing a long run (5 miles), run three minutes per mile slower than race pace and take the appropriate walk breaks, based upon pace per mile. You cannot run too slow on the long run.

- If you raced this weekend, run very easily for 4 miles after the race, 3 min/mi slower than race pace.

Sunday: If there are no significant aches and pains, jog easily for 20 minutes or take the day off!

WEEK 6

Monday: Standard warm-up, 6 CDs, 6 Acgs (no sprinting). Then, run .75 mile at goal pace (three laps around a track). It's OK to start a little faster than goal pace to get ready to run a little faster at the start of your cross-country races. Try to run each lap (or .25 mile) at the same pace. After the .75 mile time trial, walk for 5 minutes and run 2 x 400 (or .25 mi ea) about 2 seconds faster than race pace, but don't sprint! Walk half a lap between each. Then do a standard warm-down.

Tuesday: 20-30 minutes of XT is recommended (pool running is best). Runners who did the preseason training could jog a very easy 20 minutes or cross-train.

Wednesday: Speed day. Standard warm-up, then 5 CDs and 5 Acgs (no sprinting). Then, run 7 x 400 meters. Run the first 2 x 400 about 6 seconds faster than goal race pace for 1 mile. During the first 200 meters of each 400, run a little faster than workout pace. Jog for 2 minutes between each. Run the last 5 x 600s, about 4 seconds faster than goal race pace. Then, use the standard warm-down. The best venue is an accurately measured cross-country course, with stable footing (or the track).

Thursday: 4 HTs. Standard warm-up, then 3 acceleration gliders. Then, run up a hill that is 150-200 yards long. Start each hill with 4-5 strides at a jog and gradually pick up the cadence of your feet. Shorten the stride as you ascend the hill, so that your leg motion feels smooth, with no straining. Glide slightly over the top of the hill and walk for 2 minutes. Then run gently down the hill with a short to medium stride, and "coast" out onto the flat for about 50 yards (practicing downhill running form). Don't race other runners, but fine-tune your own downhill technique as you stay under control. Don't let the stride get too long. Walk for 2 minutes and repeat the cycle. Afterwards, do a standard warm-down. It is OK to run this workout on the same type of terrain as in the races, as long as the footing is stable. Those with unstable ankles should run hills on streets.

Friday: Off—you've earned a day of rest.

Saturday: Race or long run of 3.5-4 miles.

- Racers can start to run a little faster during the first 200 yards of the race (chapter 13 on race strategies). After the first mile, try a strategy of catching up with the next group ahead, running with them for 100-200 yards, then passing for the next group or individual. Ease into a steady pace until the last half-mile of the race. During the last 200 yards, try to pass one runner at a time. Don't sprint at the end, but you could gradually pick it up. Smile!

- If you're doing a long run (3.5-4 miles), be sure to read the pace guidelines (three minutes per mile slower than race pace), and take the appropriate walk breaks, based upon pace per mile. You cannot run too slowly on the long run.

- If you are racing this weekend, run very easily for 2.5-3 miles after the race, 3 min/mi slower than race pace.

Sunday: If there are no significant aches and pains, jog easily for 20 minutes or take the day off!

WEEK 7 GOAL RACE WEEK

Monday: Standard warm-up, 6 CDs, 6 Acgs (no sprinting). Then, run one half mile for time. Talk strategy with teammates and start the workout. If possible, run on the race course or similar terrain. Run the first half (.25 mi) a little faster than goal pace, practicing race strategy. Try to run the second quarter mile at goal pace. This is race practice and not competition—don't run too fast. Walk for 5 minutes and run 2 x .25 mi at about race pace. Walk about 200 yards between each. Then do a standard warm-down.

Tuesday: This should be a very easy day or a day off. XT is recommended (pool running is best for 20 minutes).

Wednesday: Speed day. This is the last speed workout before the first goal race, so save the effort for the race. Standard warm-up, then 5 CDs and 5 Acgs (no sprinting). Then, run 2 x 400 (or .25 mi) about current goal pace. Walk for 3 minutes between each. Then, use the standard warm-down. This can be run on cross-country terrain.

Thursday: 2 HTs. Standard warm-up, then 4 Acgs. Don't push the pace on these hills, just work on form and technique. Run up each hill (100-150 yards long) starting with 4-5 strides at a jog and gradually pick up the cadence of your feet. Shorten the stride as you ascend the hill, so that your leg motion feels smooth, with no straining. Glide slightly over the top of the hill and jog down gently. Afterwards, do a standard warm-down.

Friday: Off—rest for the race.

Saturday: Race!

- Racers should use the techniques that have worked well before, working with teammates when possible. Start just fast enough to get ahead of the bulk of the runners, but not so fast to leave the muscles exhausted during the last mile. Read chapter 13 on race strategies. During the second half of the race, try to pass one runner at a time to the finish. Don't save up for a final sprint—gradually pick it up during the last mile.

Sunday: If there are no significant aches and pains, jog easily for 20 minutes or take the day off!

- If you are running more races, alternate weeks 6 and 7 .

- If the season is over, congratulations. Enjoy running every other day or start training for another goal.

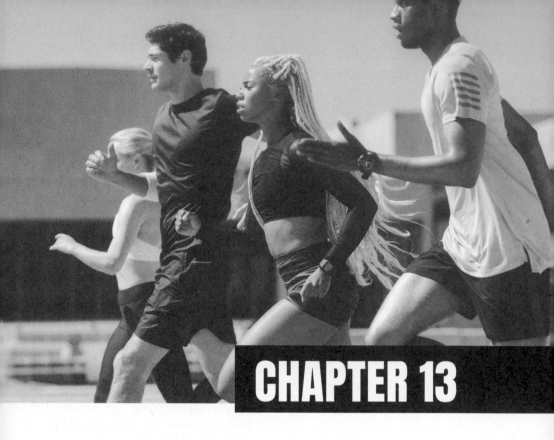

CHAPTER 13

RACING STRATEGIES FOR TEAMS AND INDIVIDUALS

Distance running is usually an individual sport. In cross-country, however, teamwork can play a big role in maximizing performance for the individual and the team. Ultimately the coach will decide upon the right strategy based upon the competitive goal for that day. When individual strengths are blended into a realistic strategy, each runner can be inspired to run faster than when running alone.

Workouts can be structured to mold a group of individuals into a team, empowering each runner to do his/her best. Setting a tone for quality and cooperation, veteran runners teach novices that they can run farther, and "dig down" on the tough days. Some teams use mantras to pull along the runners who are slowing down at the end of the workout: "Don't give up"... "Pushing beyond"... "The team needs me"... "One more step"... "We can do it"... "Together!"

A successful strategy has been to run the tough workouts in groups—gathering those who are likely to be running at the same pace in races. Workouts can be much more fun, with better quality, when runners stick together. Those who start too fast can be coached to the correct pace, while runners who lag in the middle will have support to maintain pace. At the end of each segment, everyone can find strength in the group to hang on—which reduces the slowdown. Over the season, race strategies develop and are practiced in the workouts. Most of these come from the dynamics and needs of the runners in each "pack."

KEY STRATEGIES

1. Move up at the start. During the first 200 yards, run fast enough to get out of the crowds. If an athlete doesn't start fast enough, he/she can be locked into the starting crowd, limiting movement during the rest of the race. Prepare for a faster start by running faster at the start of speed repetitions, as noted in the workout descriptions in this book. This starting pace is not a sprint, but a controlled acceleration.

2. After the first 200 yards, settle into a manageable pace until the final segment. Team members can monitor one another to reduce the chance of running too fast, too early.

3. Mid-race, teammates need to monitor who is struggling and help them. Older veterans are often a major help in this area.

4. Work together to pass one runner at a time in the second half of the race. Talk to one another: "Time to pass one runner."... "I can pass one more runner."

5. Some teams use a "buddy system." A dynamic duo can pull one another along so that both run better.

6. At the end of each workout, team members should look around and say something positive to a nearby teammate. The idea is to feel the team coming together, pulling one another, when tired.

The buddy system—enhancing performance and not holding someone back.

Experienced coaches can match up runners, so that each helps the other to avoid problems to keep going when tired. When a teammate is counting on you, you tend to dig down deeper when needed.

Example: Two runners finish at about the same time in races. Runner number one tends to go out too fast and fade; runner number two gets discouraged during the last third of the race, fades into the crowd of runners and slows down. Pairing up these two means that #1 would stay right with #2 during the first mile, allowing #2 to dictate pace. During the second half, #1 takes charge and #2 follows right behind, moving up. During the last 100-200 yards, each athlete runs as he/she wants.

Front runners. Some runners like to be in the lead, and thrive on this role. At first, this may lead to starting too fast or starting the finish "kick" too early. The repetitions listed in the training programs in this book can allow these leaders to learn proper pacing. Coaches may have to rein in the enthusiasm at the beginning, but frontrunners become great leaders during workouts and for various groups in races. Because it is so easy to go out too fast, they may slow down a bit at the end—needing team support from the "stretch runners" to achieve top performance.

Stretch runners excel at pacing themselves, saving resources for a strong finish (the home stretch). They often need to focus on the first 200 meters of the race to avoid getting behind too many runners. A strong finish can inspire team members, reviving spirits of those who were slowing down. During speed workouts, coaches can arrange groups so that front runners and stretch runners can draw off each other's strengths. Every runner can become a better finisher by progressively working harder during the last 2 repetitions of speed workouts. The object is not to sprint—but to gradually pick up the pace over the last 100-200 yards of speed repetitions, which prepares the athlete for doing this in the race itself.

CHAPTER 14

DRILLS TO MAKE RUNNING FASTER AND EASIER

The following drills have helped thousands of runners run more efficiently and faster. Each works toward a slightly different goal, but all of them reward the individual for pulling together the various running form components to eliminate extraneous motion in your feet and legs, reduce impact, use momentum, and increase the cadence or turnover of your feet and legs. Each month you will be teaching yourself to run more directly and efficiently.

When?

These should be done on a non-long-run day. It is fine, however, to do them as part of your warm-up, before a race or a speed workout. Many runners have also told me that the drills are a nice way to break up an average run that they would otherwise call "boring."

CADENCE OR TURNOVER DRILL

This is an easy drill that improves the efficiency of running, reducing effort. This pulls all the elements of good running form together at the same time. Over the weeks and months, doing this two or more times a week will naturally increase the number of steps per minute.

WHY IS CADENCE IMPORTANT?

Research shows that as distance runners get faster, the length of their stride tends to get shorter. So the key to mechanical improvement and running efficiency is more steps per minute. This drill empowers the right brain to fine-tune your form for better use of energy.

HOW TO DO THE CADENCE DRILL (CD)

1. Warm up by walking for 5 minutes, and running and walking very gently for 10 minutes.

2. Start jogging slowly for 1-2 minutes, and then time yourself for 30 seconds. During this half minute, count the number of times your left or right foot touches (each runner chooses one).

3. Walk around for a minute or so.

4. On the second 30-second drill, increase the count by 1 or 2.

5. Repeat this 3-6 more times. Each time trying to increase by 1-2 additional counts.

In the process of improving cadence or turnover, the body's internal monitoring system coordinates a series of adaptations molding the feet, legs, nervous system and timing mechanism into an efficient team:

*   Your foot touches lightly.

*   Extra, inefficient motions of the foot and leg are reduced or eliminated.

*   Less effort is spent on pushing up or moving forward, saving energy.

*   You stay lower to the ground—becoming smoother and faster.

*   The ankle becomes more efficient.

*   Abuse of weak link areas is reduced.

ACCELERATION-GLIDER DRILL (ACG)

This drill is a form of speed play, or fartlek which keeps the muscles, tendons, nerves, etc. used in running going at top capacity. By doing it regularly, you adapt the body to develop a range of speeds, with the muscle conditioning and mechanical actions to move smoothly from one to the next. The greatest benefit comes as you learn how to "glide," or coast off your momentum.

1. Done on a non-long-run day, in the middle of a shorter run, or as a warm-up for a speed session or a race.

2. Warm up with at least half a mile of easy running.

3. Many runners do the cadence drill just after the easy warm-up, and follow with acceleration-gliders. But Acgs can be done separately from the CDs, if desired.

4. Run 4-8 of them.

5. Do this at least once a week—to maintain adaptations.

6. No sprinting—never run all-out.

After teaching this drill at my one-day running schools and weekend retreats for years, I can say that most people learn better through practice when they work on the concepts of the drill—rather than the details. So just get out there and try them! When running in a group, don't compete focus on your own efficiency.

Gliding—The most important concept. This is like coasting off the momentum of a downhill run. You can do some of your gliders running down a hill if you want, but it is important to do at least two of them on the flat land.

Do this every week—As in the turnover drills, the regularity of the drill is crucial. If you're like most runners, you won't glide very far at first. Regular practice will help you glide farther and farther.

Don't sweat the small stuff—I've included a general guideline of how many steps to do with each part of the drill, but don't worry about getting any exact number of steps. It's best to get into a flow with this drill and not focus on exactly how many steps you are taking. During team workouts, don't compete with other runners. Each athlete needs to develop his/her own format.

Smooth transition—between each of the components. Each time you "shift gears" you are using the momentum of the current mode to start you into the next mode. Don't make a sudden and abrupt change, but work towards a smooth transition between modes.

HOW TO DO ACCELERATION-GLIDERS

- Start by jogging very slowly for about 15 steps.

- Then, jog faster for about 15 steps—increasing to a regular running pace for you.

- Now, over the next approximately 25 steps, gradually increase to your current race pace (no sprinting).

- OK, it's time to glide, or coast. Allow yourself to gradually slow down to a jog using momentum as long as you can. At first you may only glide for 10-15 steps. As the weeks go by, you will get up to 20, then 30 and beyond... you're gliding!

Overall Purpose: As you do this drill, every week, you will tend to run smoother during each mode of running, and overall. You may not even feel the subtle changes but your right brain finds ways of moving you along at a fairly fast pace without using much energy. This is the main object of the drill.

There will be some days when you will glide longer than others—don't worry about this. By doing this drill regularly, you will find yourself coasting or gliding down the smallest of inclines, and even for 10-20 yards on the flat, on a regular basis. Gliding conserves energy—reduces soreness, fatigue, and maintains a faster pace in races.

CHAPTER 15

HILL RUNNING TECHNIQUE AND FAQS

TOP MISTAKES MADE WHEN RUNNING HILLS IN RACES

1. Striding too long down a hill

2. Striding too long up a hill

3. Increasing the pace when running up a hill

4. Leaning too far when running up a hill

5. Leaning too far back when running down a hill

6. Leaning too far forward when running down a hill

7. Pumping the arms to get up a hill faster

8. Trying to "win the hill"

HILL RUNNING CONCEPTS

1. Keep the effort level and breathing rate consistent as you approach a hill.

2. Touch lightly as you go up the hill.

3. Very slightly reduce stride length as you run up, to maintain resiliency in the leg muscles.

4. Reduce stride to "baby steps" when needed on steep hills or long hills.

5. Monitor effort by breathing rate—try to maintain the same breathing pattern as on the flat.

6. Stay smooth when running up and running down.

7. Let gravity pull you down the hill.

8. Let cadence or turnover increase as you run down—without a great increase in stride length.

9. Encourage teammates who are struggling: don't give up and don't over-stride.

Note: The next chapter will detail how to run up hills in a workout.

UPHILL RUNNING FORM DURING RACES AND AVERAGE RUNS

- Start with a comfortable stride—fairly short.

- As you go up the hill, shorten the stride.

- Touch lightly with your feet.

- Maintain a body posture that is perpendicular to the horizontal (upright, not leaning forward or back).

- Pick up the turnover of your feet as you go up and over the top.

- Keep adjusting stride so that the leg muscles don't tighten up—you want them as resilient as possible.

- Relax as you go over the top of the hill, and glide (or coast) on the downside, minimizing effort.

CHAPTER 16

HILL TRAINING FOR STRENGTH AND RACE PREPARATION

Hill training strengthens the legs for running better than any other activity I know. At the same time it can help you maximize use of an efficient stride length, increase leg speed, and improve your ability to run hills in races. The hill training workouts are not designed to lead to exhaustion. They should gently introduce the feet, legs and cardiovascular system to faster running, while improving the capacity to run up hills in races.

THE HILL WORKOUT

- Walk for 2-3 minutes.

- Jog and walk to a hill—about 10 minutes. Beginners or comebackers should jog a minute and walk a minute (a longer warm-up is fine) during the first few weeks of training of the 10-minute warm-up.

- Do 4 acceleration-gliders (don't sprint). These are listed in chapter 14.

- Reverse this warm-up as your warm-down.

- Choose a hill with a moderate grade—steep hills often cause problems.

- Run up the hill for 5 seconds, and then down for 5 seconds, gently. Walk for 10-15 seconds. Repeat this 5-10 times. This finalizes the warm-up.

- Walk for 3-4 minutes.

- Run the first few steps of each hill acceleration at a jog, then gradually pick up the turnover of the feet as you go up the hill.

- Get into a comfortable rhythm, so that you can gradually increase this turnover (# of steps per minute) as you go up the hill.

- Keep shortening stride length as you go up the hill.

- It's OK to huff and puff at the top of the hill (due to increased turnover and running uphill, but don't let the legs get over-extended, or feel exhausted).

- Run over the top of the hill by at least 10 steps.

- Jog back to the top of the hill and walk down to recover between the hills. Walk as much as you need for complete recovery after each hill.

HILL WORKOUT RUNNING FORM

- Start with a comfortable stride—fairly short.

- As you go up the hill, shorten the stride.

- Touch lightly with your feet.

- Maintain a body posture that is perpendicular to the horizontal (upright, not leaning forward or back).

- Pick up the turnover of your feet as you go up and over the top.

- Keep adjusting stride so that the leg muscles don't tighten up—you want them as resilient as possible.

- Relax as you go over the top of the hill, and glide (or coast) a bit on the downside.

HILL TRAINING STRENGTHENS LOWER LEGS AND IMPROVES RUNNING FORM

The incline of the hill forces your legs to work harder as you go up. The extra work up the incline and the faster turnover builds strength. By taking an easy walk between the hills, and an easy day afterward, the lower leg muscles rebuild stronger. Over several months, the improved strength allows you to support your body weight farther forward on your feet. An extended range of motion of the ankle and Achilles tendon results in a "bonus" extension of the foot forward—with no increase in effort. You will run faster without working harder. What a deal!

RUNNING FASTER ON HILLS IN RACES

Once you train yourself to run with efficient hill form, you'll run faster with increased turnover on the hill workouts. This prepares you to do the same in races. You won't run quite as fast in a race as in your workouts. But through hill training you train yourself to run faster than you used to run up the same hill on a race course.

Hill technique in a race is the same as in workouts: keep shortening your stride as you move up the hill. Monitor your respiration rate: don't huff and puff more than you were doing on the flat. As runners improve their hill technique in races, they find that a shorter and quicker stride reduces effort while increasing speed. The technique isright for the individual when there is no increase in breathing rate even when the turnover rate is increased slightly.

 Note: On your long runs and easy running days, just jog up hills, don't run faster up the hill. If your breathing is increasing on a hill, reduce effort and stride length until your respiration is as it was on the flat ground—or take more frequent walk breaks on the flat.

DOWNHILL FORM

- Maintain a light touch of the foot.

- Use an average stride—or quick shuffle.

- Keep feet low to the ground.

- Let gravity pull you down the hill.

- Turnover of the feet will pick up.

- Try to glide (or coast) quickly down the hill.

BIGGEST MISTAKES: TOO LONG A STRIDE, BOUNCING TOO MUCH

Even when the stride is one or two inches too long, your downhill speed can get out of control. If you are bouncing more than an inch or two off the ground, you run the risk of pounding your feet, having to use your quads to slow down (producing soreness) and creating hamstring soreness due to over-stride. The best indicator of over-stride is having tight hamstrings (big muscle behind your upper leg), and sore quads the next day. Using a quick and slightly shorter stride can allow one to run just as fast downhill as with a long stride, without sore quads, sore shins or aggravated hamstrings.

CHAPTER 17

CROSS-TRAINING: GETTING BETTER AS YOU REST THE LEGS

The best item you can insert into a successful speed training program to reduce injury... is an extra rest day or two. The hard work of running involves lifting your body off the ground, and then absorbing the shock. If you are running seven days a week— especially when doing speedwork—you may not allow the damage to be repaired.

Once runners get into a speed program, and start to improve, some will try to sneak in an extra day or two on the days that should be "off." They often feel, mistakenly, that they can gain performance with an additional day, or that they are losing fitness when they take a day off. This perception does not match up with reality. Even with easy and short runs (on days that should be off) the legs cannot fully recover—especially from speed workouts. These short runs on "rest days" give you the so-called "junk miles" which increase fatigue and risk of injury.

CROSS-TRAINING ACTIVITIES

When an athlete is on the edge of over-training or getting injured, the best strategy is to run one day, and cross-train the next. Cross-training simply means "alternative exercise" to running. Your goal is to find exercises that give you a good feeling of exertion, but do not fatigue the workhorses of running: calf muscles, Achilles tendon, feet.

When injured, cross-training can often maintain most of the running adaptations, while allowing for healing. Many runners have reported to me that they lost little or no performance during a 1-2 week "injury vacation" because they simulated their running workouts through aqua-jogging.

EASE INTO A NEW EXERCISE!

1. Start with 5 easy minutes of exercise, rest for 20 or more minutes and do 5 more easy minutes.

2. Take a day of rest before doing the exercise again (you can do a different exercise the next day).

3. Increase by 2-3 additional minutes each session.

4. Once you have increased to two 15-minute sessions, you could shift to one 22 to 25-minute session and increase by 2-3 more minutes per session if you wish.

5. During the first few weeks of a new exercise, it's best to do no exercise the day before a long run, a very hard speed session, or a race. Later in the season, it is usually OK to aqua-jog for a few minutes on those days.

6. To maintain conditioning in each alternative exercise, do one session each week of 10 minutes or more once you reach that amount. If you have the time, you can cross-train on all of your days off from running—except listed in #5 above.

7. The maximum cross-training is up to the individual. As long as you are feeling fine for the rest of the day and have no trouble with your runs the next day, the length of your cross-training should not be a problem.

WATER RUNNING (AQUA-JOGGING) CAN IMPROVE YOUR RUNNING FORM

All of us have little flips and side motions of our legs that interfere with our running efficiency. During a water running workout, the resistance of the water forces your legs to find a more efficient path. In addition, several leg muscles are strengthened which can help to keep legs on a smoother path when they get tired at the end of a long run or tiring speed workout.

HERE'S HOW!

You'll need a flotation belt for this exercise. The product "aqua jogger" is designed to float you off the bottom of the pool, and on most runners, tightens so that it is close to the body. There are many other ways to keep you floating, including water ski float belts and life jackets. You can see more about this at *www.JeffGalloway.com*.

Get in the deep end of the pool and move your legs through a running motion. This means little or no knee lift, kicking out slightly in front of you, and bringing the leg behind, with the foot coming up behind you. As in running, your lower leg should be parallel with the horizontal during the back-kick.

If you are not feeling much exertion, you're probably lifting the knees too high and moving your legs through a small range of motion. To get the benefit, an extended running motion is needed.

It's important to do water running once a week to keep the adaptations that you have gained. If you miss a week, you should drop back a few minutes from your previous session. If you miss more than 3 weeks, start back at two 5- to 8-minute sessions.

NORDIC TRACK

This exercise machine simulates the motion used in cross-country skiing. It is one of the better cross-training modes for running because it uses a large number of leg and back muscle cells.

ROWING MACHINE

There are a number of different types of rowing machines. Some work the legs a bit too hard for runners, but most allow you to use a wide variety of lower and upper body muscle groups.

CYCLING

Indoor or outdoor cycling won't help your running performance but shouldn't hurt it either. If you are in a spinning class, in which you are standing and pushing on the pedals, you will be using the calf muscle. This should be avoided on a rest day from running but could be done as a second workout, on a running day.

ELLIPTICAL

Because you don't use the calf muscles on this machine, this is an appropriate exercise on a non-running day. While this will not improve your running performance, it can give you a good cardiovascular workout on a day when you can't run for some reason.

CROSS-TRAINING FOR THE UPPER BODY

WEIGHT TRAINING

While weight work is not a great fat-burning exercise, and does not directly benefit running, it can be done on non-running days, or on running days, after a run. There is a wide range of different ways to build strength. If interested, find a coach that can help you build strength in the muscle groups you wish to be strengthened. Weight training for the legs is not recommended.

NOTE: I do two exercises that have helped me maintain the strength of my postural muscles.

The Crunch—lie on your back, on carpet or any padded surface. Lift your head and upper back slightly off the floor. Go through a narrow range of motion so that you feel your abdominal muscles contracting almost constantly. Start with a few seconds of these, and build up to 30-60 seconds, done 3-5 times a day (one or two days a week).

Arm running—while standing, with hand-held weights (milk jugs, etc) move your arms through a wide range of motion you would use when running—maybe slightly more than usual. Keep the weights close to the body. Start with a few reps, and gradually build up to 3-5 sets of 10. Pick a weight that is challenging enough so that you feel exertion at the end of a set of 10. You don't want to have to struggle during the last few reps.

DON'T DO THESE ON NON-RUNNING DAYS!

The following exercises will tire the muscles used for running and keep them from recovering between run days. If you really like to do any of these exercises, you can do them after a run, on a short running day.

- Stair machines
- Stair aerobics
- Weight training for the leg muscles
- Power walking—especially on a hilly course
- Spinning classes (on a bicycle) in which you stand up on the pedals and push

CHAPTER 18

THE GALLOWAY RUN-WALK-RUN METHOD

Taking the right frequency of walk breaks on long runs allow runners to recover faster, avoid injuries and perform better in speed workouts and races.

Running continuously causes the muscles to fatigue more rapidly—primarily because the muscles must be used mile after mile—without relief. If you break the cycle of continuous use by walking early enough, you allow the muscles to rebound, so that they can go farther or faster at the end. This process gives you an extraordinary degree of control over the amount of fatigue you put on your legs.

WALK BEFORE YOU GET TIRED ON LONG RUNS

If you want to have leg strength at the end, and recover fast, you need to take walk breaks from the beginning—before you start to get tired. With each walk in the first third of the run, you increase bounce of your muscles at the end—and you'll decrease leg fatigue. The most important walk break is the first one. Many runners have trouble with this and don't walk until they're tired. As a result, they have trouble starting back up from their break—or don't recover quickly.

YOU CAN CONTROL YOUR FATIGUE!

By using a ratio of running and walking that works for you, you'll conserve energy, keep the muscles resilient and strong, and recover quickly. Having a strategy that works so well bestows a mental confidence which will help you later in a challenging run. After long training runs, you want to recover quickly so that you can get on to your other training. Walk breaks speed recovery faster than anything I've found. There is no need to reach the end of a long run, feeling exhausted—your legs stay fresh by taking liberal walk breaks, for you, on that day.

WALK BREAKS ...

- Give you control over your level of strength at the end of a run.

- Erase fatigue.

- Push back your fatique wall.

- Allow for endorphins to collect during each walk break—you feel good!

- Break up the distance into manageable units ("one more minute").

- Speed up the recovery of your leg muscles.

- Reduce the chance of aches, pains and injury.

- Allow you to feel good afterward—carrying on the rest of your day without debilitating fatigue.

- Give you all of the speed or endurance of each session—without the pain.

- Allow injured runners to make a quicker comeback.

- Help you run faster by allowing you to have better quality in the upcoming speed workouts!

A SHORT BUT QUICK WALKING STRIDE

It's better to walk with a short stride. There has been some irritation of the shins when runners or walkers maintain a stride that is too long. Through practice, you can increase the pace of your walk as you develop a smooth, quick stride, through quick turnover.

A LONG RUN WITH WALK BREAKS GIVES YOU THE SAME ENDURANCE

On long runs, the distance is the only thing that matters. You get the same endurance whether you take walk breaks or not.

Your choice:

* A long run of 5 miles running continuously gives 5 miles of endurance.

* A long run with walk breaks gives 5 miles of endurance, but allows for much quicker recovery, and more enjoyment.

RUNNING CONTINUOUSLY CAN COMPROMISE A TIME GOAL

Runners who do not take walk breaks risk not fully recovering from the long run. The residual fatigue is carried into the speed sessions, and compounded by other long runs. As the lingering fatigue builds up, tired muscles can't deliver the performance in the race that they could have done with walk breaks.

How to use walk breaks on long runs

1. Look at the following schedule as a guide (you can take them more often with no penalty).

2. Be sure to take the walk breaks from the beginning.

3. When in doubt, take the walk breaks more often.

Pace/mile	Run-Walk-Run strategy
8 min/mile	run 4 min/walk 30 seconds
8:30 min/mile	run 3 min/walk 30 seconds
9 min/mile	run 2 min/walk 30 seconds
9:30 min/mile	run 1:45-2 min/walk 30 seconds
10 min/mile	run 90 seconds/walk 30 seconds
10:30 min/mile	run 75 seconds/walk 30 seconds
11 min/mile	run 75-60 seconds/walk 30 seconds
12 min/mile	run 60 seconds/walk 30 seconds
13 min/mile	run 30 seconds/walk 30 seconds or 20/20
14 min/mile	30/30 or 20/20 or 15/15 or run 20/walk 30
15 min/mi	run 15 seconds/walk 30 seconds
16 min/mi	run 10 seconds/walk 30 seconds

HOW TO KEEP TRACK OF THE WALK BREAKS

Try out our interval timer featured on our website, www.jeffgalloway.com. But most smart watches and phones have features that will allow you track your intervals.

WALK BREAKS IN RACES?

Each year I hear from a growing number of beginning or "comeback" cross-country runners who run faster when they add short walk breaks during their race. If you are running at 8 min/mi or slower you will probably benefit from a short walk break every half mile or so when the race distance is one mile or more. Many find that short walk breaks on tough hills, during the beginning of the season, allow them to be strong to the finish.

Don't be afraid to experiment with walk breaks.

CHAPTER 19

INJURY PREVENTION AND CARE

WHY DO MICRO-TEARS ACCUMULATE?

- Constant use (insufficient rest between stress workouts)
- Uneven terrain
- Prior damage
- Speedwork
- Too many races
- Doing something different
- Sudden increase of workload
- Inadequate rest between workouts
- Not enough walk breaks during long runs
- Stretching

COMMON CAUSES OF INJURIES

It's a physiological fact that the constant use of a muscle, tendon, joint, etc., without a break, will result in earlier fatigue and reduced work potential. Continuing to run when the muscle is extremely fatigued, increases the quantity of micro-tears dramaticallly and is a major cause of injury.

By pacing conservatively and by inserting walk breaks early and often in long runs and speed workouts, each runner will gain a great deal of control over the fatigue process, while allowing muscles, tendons, feet, joints, etc. to repair damage and maintain capacity. This lowers the chance of breakdown, by significantly reducing the accumulating damage that leads to injury.

NOTE: **This information is given as one runner to another and is not intended to be medical advice. See a doctor for medical issues.**

Here are some "tools" that can give you control over your aches and pains:

* Be sensitive to weak links and let aggravations heal by strategic rest and treatment immediately when a potential injury is experienced.

* Run long runs at least 3 minutes per mile slower than current race pace.

* Speedwork segments are paced according to the recommendations in this book.

* Run speedwork and long runs at the right pace for YOU and not that of faster runners.

* Gradually increase the speed and distance of workouts—no sudden increases.

* Take two or three days off from running per week (read chapter 17 on cross-training).

* Take the full rest interval between speed segments recommended in this book.

* Take all walk breaks recommended on long runs, based upon pace per mile.

* Avoid stretching weak links—stretching aggravates or causes many injuries.

* Don't try to change your running form significantly.

* Shoes—get good fitting advice from the experts in a good running store.

* Gradually break in a new shoe—don't shift suddenly from a very worn shoe to a new one.

* Run on stable terrain. If weak links hurt, shift to stable terrain (track, road or bike trail).

AGGRAVATING FACTORS

- Prior damage—especially due to accident trauma, football, soccer, skiing, etc. It may not be possible for all of the damage to be repaired. In most cases, training adjustments can be made

NOTE: **Studies show that runners have healthier joints and fewer orthopedic complaints than non-runners after decades of running. See my book RUNNING UNTIL YOU'RE 100 for more information.**

- Speed—Speed training and frequent racing increases stress on the weak links significantly. I have found individual training adjustments can often allow for continued training, but sometimes there needs to be a "vacation from speed" for a week or two.

- Stride length—longer strides increase risk. A shorter stride may not slow you down if you will increase cadence or turnover. (See chapter 14 for the drills)

- Bounce off the ground—the higher the bounce, the more stress on feet, legs and joints. The higher the bounce, the more shock to be absorbed upon landing. Stay low to the ground, touching lightly.

- Stretching—I have heard from thousands of runners who have been injured or had injuries aggravated by stretching. In general, I do not recommend stretching. There are individuals who benefit from certain stretches, however. Be careful if you choose to stretch. Stretching is not generally found to be beneficial as a warm-up or warm-down activity, and causes injuries when done at these times. Trying to "stretch out" fatigue-induced tightness often results in injury and prolonged recovery.

NOTE: **Those who have iliotibial band injury can often get relief from a few specific stretches that act as a "quick fix" to keep you running. Even when doing these, be careful. The foam roller can help move "bio junk" out of the damaged area, and the BFF massager can improve blood flow, healing and speed recovery. (See info on the BFF at www.Phidippides.com.)**

- Continuing to work out when an injury has begun can dramatically increase the damage in a few minutes. It is always better to stop the exercise immediately if there is an indication that you have an injury.

- Avoid certain exercises that aggravate your weak links (individual in nature).

- The "toe squincher." Everyone should do this exercise every day to reduce/eliminate the chance of having a plantar fascia injury—or other foot problems. Point your foot down and contract the muscles in the forefoot/midfoot region. This strengthens the many little muscles in your feet that will provide extra support.

HOW DO YOU KNOW IF YOU ARE INJURED?

Continuing to exercise when you feel that you might have an injury puts you at great risk of an extended layoff from running. In most cases that I've monitored, when I suspect that there is an injury, it usually is an injury. Be sensitive to your weak links. When you notice any of the following symptoms, take at least a day or two off from running.

- Inflammation—swelling, puffiness or thickening

- Loss of function—the area doesn't work correctly or move normally

- Pain—if the pain does not go away as you get warmed up and walk slowly, or the pain increases, STOP!

YOU CAN TAKE 5 DAYS OFF FROM RUNNING WITH NO SIGNIFICANT LOSS IN CONDITIONING

It is always better to err on the conservative side of injury repair. If you take an extra day off at the beginning of an injury you won't lose any conditioning. But if you continue training with an injury, you may increase the healing time by a week or a month for each day trying to "push through pain."

QUICK ACTION CAN REDUCE RECOVERY TIME NEEDED

Some minor irritation may require just one day off from running. As the pain level increases, so does the need for more recovery days.

HOW TO TRAIN WHILE INJURED (IF INJURY ALLOWS)

- Get the OK from your doctor to continue training.

- Stay below the threshold of further irritation.

- Work out every other day.

- Insert walk breaks/shuffle breaks into runs.

- Avoid faster running or gently ease back into faster running.

- Don't stretch (unless you have certain stretches that work for you and don't hurt you).

- Long run endurance can often be maintained by walking the distance of the long one when injured.

- Run in the water for the number of minutes you would be running on land (see chapter 17 on cross-training).

REDUCING RISK OF SPEED INJURIES

- Warm up—start very slowly, gradually increase some accelerations, and ease into the workout.

- Run the first and the last repetition more slowly than the others.

- Don't race the last repetition.

- Rest between repetitions—when you have a history of speed injuries, take more rest.

- Some runners are more prone to injury than others. Athletes need to tell the coach when there might be an injury. Coaches may need to rearrange groups to reduce injury risk on certain runners.

STAYING IN SHAPE WHEN INJURED

- Many running injuries will heal while you continue to run, if you stay below the threshold of further irritation. Talk to your doctor about this issue to ensure that the healing has started and that you are not irritating the injury as you start back.

- Cross-training—Pick an activity that does not aggravate the injury. Water running is the best for maintaining running conditioning. To hold current endurance, schedule a long water run session that is the same number of water running minutes you would spend running your current long run. Some runners have been able to maintain speed conditioning by doing a speed running workout in the water, once a week.

- Swimming, cycling, etc. are good for overall fitness, but don't have a lot of direct benefit to runners.

- Activities to avoid: Anything that irritates the injury.

- If you can walk, walk for at least an hour, every other day.

HOW TO RETURN TO RUNNING

- Check with your doctor to ensure that enough healing has occurred to begin running again.

- Stay below the threshold of irritation. You want to see progress, week by week, in reduction of pain.

- Stay in touch with your doctor and ask questions if you suspect that you are aggravating the injury.

- Avoid exercising if you are "favoring" the injured area, or limping. Running in an abnormal way can result in a worse injury in another location.

- If you haven't been running, start by walking. Build up to a 30-minute walk.

- Insert small segments of running into a walk (run 5-10 seconds, walk the rest of the minute). If there is no aggravation, you could increase 5 seconds on the running segment while decreasing 5 seconds on the walking segment—after using each new ratio for at least 2 workouts.

- Avoid anything that could aggravate the injured area.

- First increase should be in the duration of the long run, by 5-10 minutes, every other week. Keep the run-walk-run ratio mostly walking for the first week before increasing.

INJURIES FROM RUNNING FORM MISTAKES

While the body adapts and adjusts to the running motion, workouts or races that are long and strenuous can result in irregularities in our normal form. Since the body is not adapted to these "wobbles", weak links can be irritated. Continued use and using an unaccustomed range of motion can lead to injury. Here are some of the common ones. For more information see my book RUNNING INJURIES: CARE & PREVENTION and consult a knowledgeable sports medicine doctor.

TROUBLESHOOTING FORM-RELATED INJURIES

Lower back—Caused by forward lean, over-stride, too few walk breaks Neck pain—Caused by forward lean, head placed too far forward or back Hamstring pain—Caused by striding too long, stretching

Shin pain on front—Caused by stride length too long, especially on downhills or at end of run

Shin pain on inside—Caused by over pronation, uneven terrain Achilles—Caused by stretching, speedwork, overpronation

Calf pain—Caused by stretching, speedwork, inadequate number of walk breaks on long run

Knee pain—Caused by too few walk breaks, overpronation, speedwork, extended stride

THE "SHUFFLE"

The most efficient and gentle running form is a "shuffle". The feet stay next to the ground, touching lightly with a relatively short stride. When running at the most relaxed range of the shuffling motion, the ankle mechanism does a great deal of the work, and little effort is required from the calf muscle. But when the foot pushes harder and bounces more, and the stride increases, there are often more aches, pains and injuries.

SPEEDWORK INCREASES INJURY RISK

Time goal runners need to run faster in some workouts, and this means some increase in stride length, greater bounce and foot pushing. By gradually increasing the intensity of speed training (with sufficient rest intervals and rest days between) feet and legs can adapt. But there is still a risk of injury. Be sensitive to your weak links and don't keep running if there is the chance that you may have the beginnings of an injury. A gentle increase in the beginning of the season can significantly reduce risk.

CORRECT POSTURE CAN REDUCE ACHES AND PAINS

Posture is an individual issue. Most of the runners I've worked with find that an upright posture (like a "puppet on a string") is best in all ways. When runners use a forward lean there is a tendency to develop lower back pain and neck pain. A small minority of runners naturally run with a forward lean with no problems. In this case, one should run the way that is most natural.

Suggestions for running smoother, reducing irritation to weak links

- Feet—low to the ground, using a light touch of the foot.

- Try not to bounce more than an inch off the ground.

- Let your feet move the way that is natural for them. If you tend to land on your heel and roll forward, do so.

- If you have motion control issues, a foot device can provide minor correction to bring you into alignment and avoid irritating a weak link. A supportive shoe is also needed.

- Legs—Maintain a gentle stride that allows your leg muscles to stay relaxed. In general, it's better to have a shorter stride, and focus on quicker turnover if you want to speed up.

- Water running can help in reducing flips and turns of the feet and legs—which sometimes cause injuries, aches and pains. With a flotation device, run in the deep end of the pool so that your foot does not touch the bottom. Even one session of 15 minutes once a week can be beneficial.

CRAMPS IN THE MUSCLES

At some point, most people who run will experience at least an occasional cramp. These muscle contractions usually occur in the feet or the calf muscles and may come during a run, or they may hit at random afterward. Very commonly, they will occur at night, or when you are sitting around at your desk or watching TV in the afternoon or evening. When severe cramps occur during a run, you will have to stop or significantly slow down.

Most common cause of muscle cramping is overexertion of the muscle, especially during the first mile or so. A slower warm-up often helps, as does a slower pace at the beginning of a workout. Running too hard on hilly terrain is also a cause. Bouncing too high on each stride can increase the tendency to cramp. Stay low to the ground.

Cramps vary in severity. Most are mild but some can grab so hard that they shut down the muscles and hurt when they seize up. Light massage can relax the muscle and allow it to get back to work. Stretching usually increases the damage from the cramp, tearing the muscle fibers, according to my experience.

Most cramps are due to overuse—doing more than in the recent past, or continuing to put yourself at your limit, especially in warm weather. Look at the pace and distance of your runs and workouts in your training journal to see if you have been running too far, or too fast, or both. Remember to adjust long run pace for heat: 20-30 sec a mile slower for each 5 degrees (F) of temperature increase above 60°F—or 20 sec/ kilometer slower for every 2 degrees C of temperature increase above 14°C.

- Continuous running increases cramping. Taking walk breaks more often can reduce or eliminate them. Numerous runners, who used to cramp on long runs when they ran continuously, stopped cramping with a 30-second walk after 1-3 minutes of running.

- During hot weather, a good electrolyte beverage (consumed during the day, during the 24 hours after a long or hard run) can help to replace the fluids and electrolytes that your body loses in sweating. Accelerade has been the most effective in my experience. Drink approximately 6-8 oz every 2-4 hours, throughout the day.

- On hot days, waiting for the cross-country race, continuous sweating can push your sodium levels too low and trigger a fatigue cramp more quickly. If this happens regularly, a buffered salt tablet has helped greatly—a product like Succeed. If you have any blood pressure or other sodium issues, check with your doctor first.

Here are several ways of dealing with cramps:

1. Take a longer and more gentle warm-up.
2. Shorten your run segment—or take walk breaks more often.
3. Slow down your walk, and walk more.
4. Take a longer warm-up during speed sessions.
5. Look at any other exercise that could be causing the cramps.
6. Take a buffered salt tablet during your long workouts (follow the directions on the label).
7. Don't push off as hard, or bounce as high off the ground.
8. Shorten stride length.
9. During speed workouts on hot days, walk more during the rest interval.

EXERCISES THAT CAN PREVENT/TREAT INJURIES

PLANTAR FASCIA AND FOOT INJURIES— TOE SQUINCHER

This strengthens the many muscles in the foot promoting a strong push off, reducing foot fatigue, and reducing foot damage. Point your foot down and contract the muscles of the foot, which will cause the toes to curl in. Keep the contraction until the foot cramps. This can be done when wearing shoes or not, 15-20 times a day.

BACK AND SHOULDER SORENESS AND PAIN—ARM RUNNING/THE CRUNCH

Holding dumbbells (hand held weights) in each hand, go through a slightly exaggerated motion one would use when running, for a set of 10 (one left and one right equals one repetion). Pick a weight that is heavy enough so that you feel you have strengthened the shoulder and neck muscles, but not so much that you struggle to finish the last two repetitions.

FOAM ROLLER WITH BFF MASSAGE

This is the best treatment I've found for speeding the healing of the IT band. Use a cylinder of dense foam (illustrated on www.jeffgalloway.com). Lie down on your side, where the IT pain is felt. Rest your body weight on the roller and move your body (pressing down on the roller) with your hands so that you're rolling from below the pain site to just above it. Roll for 5 minutes before the run, 5 minutes after the run and 5 minutes before bed at night (probably the most effective). After each foam roller treatment, use the BFF massager for 5 minutes (see info on the BFF at www.Phidippides.com).

ICE MASSAGE FOR ACHILLES AND OTHER TENDONS NEXT TO THE SKIN

Freeze a paper cup or Styrofoam cup. Peel off the outer layer at the top to form a popsicle of ice Rub the ice constantly over the tendon for 15 minutes. The area should be numb after the treatment.

NIGHT TREATMENTS MAY HELP MORE THAN OTHERS

Experts tell me that most of the healing occurs overnight. If you perform one of these treatments before you go to bed, you may speed up the healing process.

PREVENTING SPEED INJURIES

Running faster than your "comfortable" pace for that day will increase injury risk. The farther and faster you go in a speed workout or race, the greater the risk. But since you must run faster during some workouts to run faster in races, here are some ways of reducing this risk.

- Warm up thoroughly:

  1. Walk for 3 minutes.

  2. Then run and walk for 10 minutes using a lot more frequent walk breaks than you use in a normal run. If you use a 3-1 normally, do the first 10 minutes at a 1-1 (run a minute and walk a minute).

  3. Next, run for 5 minutes starting slowly and gradually picking up the pace to a normal short run pace.

  4. Finally, do 4-8 acceleration gliders: run for 15 steps at a slow jog, then 15 steps at a faster jog, gradually accelerate to workout pace over 15 steps and then glide or coast back down to a jog over 30-40 steps. Take a 30-60 second walk/jog and repeat. After 4-8 of these, walk for 2-3 minutes and start the workout or line up for the race.

- Ease into the speed for the day. Run the first repetition at a pace that is 15 sec/mile slower than you want to run in the middle of the workout. Run the first mile of your race about 5-10 seconds slower than your goal pace for that race.

- Insert walk breaks from the beginning. These will vary based upon pace and race distance or repetition distance.

- Walk to recover between speed repetitions. The amount of walking will vary depending upon the distance of the goal race and the pace. It is better to err on the side of walking longer if you feel the need early, there are more aches than usual, or the temperature is above 70°F (19°C).

- Never run through pain, swelling, or loss of function—stop the workout. After walking for a few minutes, if the pain goes away, resume the workout with caution. If you start to limp in any way, stop.

- Stay smooth even when tired. If your form is changing due to fatigue, slow down or stop.

- Run the last repetition 15 sec/mi slower than the pace of the middle repetitions. Racing or sprinting during the last repetition produces many injuries.

- Don't run too many speed workouts, races, or other fast runs too close together.

If you are sensitive to your weak links, take the appropriate walk breaks and rest days, stop training when there could be an injury, and treat a damaged body part, you may avoid all serious injuries. This will bestow the greatest reward from running: enjoyment of every run.

CHAPTER 20

DEALING WITH THE HEAT

Backing off the pace early on a hot day can mean a higher finish place.

If you slow down a little on a warm day, you can finish strong, passing runners at the end. That seems obvious, but many runners "lose it" at the beginning of a hot race. The result is a much slower time—because of the inevitable slowdown at the end. For every second you run too fast during the first mile of a race on a hot day, you can usually expect to run 2-10 seconds slower at the end.

When you exercise strenuously in even moderate heat (above 60°F/14°C), you raise core body temperature. Most beginning runners will see the internal temperature rise above 55°F/12°C. This triggers a release of blood into the capillaries of your skin to help cool you down. This diversion reduces the blood supply available to your exercising muscles, meaning that you will have less blood and less oxygen delivered to the power source that moves you forward— and less blood to move out the waste products from these work sites. As the waste builds up in the muscle, you will slow down.

So the bad news is that in warm weather you are going to feel worse and run slower. The worse news is that working too hard on a hot day could result in a very serious condition called heat disease. Make sure that you read the section on this health problem at the end of this chapter. The good news is that you can adapt to these conditions to some extent, as you learn the best time of the day, clothing, and other tricks to keep you cool. But it is always better to back off or stop running at the first sign that you or one of your teammates may be coming into this condition. The following are proven ways of avoiding heat adversity.

RUNNING THE LONG WORKOUTS DURING SUMMER HEAT

1. Run before the sun gets above the horizon. Get up early during the warm months and you will avoid most of the dramatic stress from the sun. This is particularly a problem in humid areas. Early morning is usually the coolest time of the day, also. Without having to deal with the sun, most runners can gradually adapt to heat. At the very least, your runs will be more enjoyable than later in the day. Note: Be sure to take care of safety issues.

2. If you must run when the sun is up, pick a shady course. Shade provides a significant relief in areas of low humidity, and some relief in humid environments.

3. In areas of low humidity, it's usually cool during the evening and night. In humid environments there may not be much relief. The coolest time of the day when it's humid is just before dawn.

4. Use a pool for some short runs. Water running can be a replacement for a short and easy run.

5. Use a treadmill during preseason short run days. Some alternate segments on hot days: 5-10 minutes outdoor, and 5-10 minutes indoor.

6. Don't wear a hat! You lose most of your body heat through the top of your head. Covering the head will cause a quicker internal buildup of heat.

7. Wear light clothing, but not cotton. Many of the new, technical fibers (polypro, Coolmax, Drifit, etc.) will move moisture away from your skin, producing a cooling effect. Cotton soaks up the sweat, making the garment heavier as it sticks to your skin. This means that you won't receive as much of a cooling effect as that provided by the tech products.

8. Pour water over your head. Evaporation not only helps the cooling process—it makes you feel cooler. This psychological boost which can be huge. If you can bring along ice water with you, you will feel a lot cooler as you squirt some regularly over the top of your head—using a pop-top water bottle.

9. Do your short runs in installments. It is fine, on a hot day that is scheduled for an easy run, to put in your 30 minutes by doing 10 in the morning, 10 at noon and 10 at night. The long runs and speed workouts should be done from start to finish—but more rest can be taken between speed reps, and you may break up the distance when it's hot (running twice as many 400s if you were scheduled for 800 meter repeats).

10. Sunscreen—a mixed review. Some runners will need to protect themselves. Some products, however, produce a coating on the skin, reducing the cooling effect of perspiration and producing an increase in body temperature buildup. Find a product that doesn't block the pores.

11. 1 Drink 6-8 oz of a sports drink like Accelerade or water, at least every 2 hours, or when thirsty, throughout the day during hot weather (not necessarily when running).

12. Look at the clothing thermometer in chapter 22. Wear loose fitting garments that have some texture in the fabric. Texture will limit or prevent the perspiration from causing the fabric to cling and stick to the skin.

13. When the temperature is above 100°F, you have my permission to rearrange your running shoes—preferably in an air conditioned environment.

HOT WEATHER SLOWDOWN FOR LONG RUNS

As the temperature rises above 55°F (12°C), your body starts to build up heat, but most runners aren't significantly slowed until 60°F. If you make the adjustments early, you won't have to suffer later and slow down a lot more at that time. The baseline for this information is 60°F or 14°C.

Between 60 and 64°F—slow down 20-30 seconds per mile slower than you would run at 60°F
Between 14 and 16.5°C, slow down 15-20 seconds per kilometer than you would run at 14°C
Between 65 and 69°F—Slow down one minute per mile slower than you would run at 60°F
Between 17 and 19.5°C—slow down 40 seconds per kilometer slower than you would run at 14°C
Between 70 and 74°F—slow down 1:30 per mile slower than you would run at 60°F
Between 20 and 22°C—slow down one minute per kilometer slower than you would run at 14°C
Between 75 and 79°F—slow down 2 minutes per mile slower than you would run at 60°F
Between 22.5 and 25°C—slow down 1:20 per kilometer slower than you would run at 14°C
Above 80°F and 25°C—be careful, take extra precautions to avoid heat disease
Or... exercise indoors
Or... arrange your shoes next to the air conditioner

HEAT DISEASE ALERT!

While it is unlikely that you will push yourself into heat disease, the longer you are exercising in hot (and/or humid) conditions, the more you increase the likelihood of this dangerous medical situation. That's why I recommend breaking up your exercise into short segments when it's hot, if you must run outdoors for your short runs. Be sensitive to your reactions to the heat, and those of the runners around you. When one of the symptoms is present, this is normally not a major problem unless there is significant distress. But when several are experienced, take action because heat disease can lead to death. It's always better to be conservative: stop the workout and cool off.

Symptoms:

- Intense heat buildup in the head
- General overheating of the body
- Significant headache
- Significant nausea
- General confusion and loss of concentration
- Loss of muscle control
- Excessive sweating and then cessation of sweating
- Clammy skin
- Excessively rapid breathing
- Muscle cramps
- Feeling faint
- Unusual heart beat or rhythm

Risk factors:

- Viral or bacterial infection
- Taking medication—especially cold medicines, diuretics, medicines for diarrhea, antihistamines, atropine, scopolamine, tranquilizers, even cholesterol and blood pressure medications. Check with your doctor on medication issues—especially when running in hot weather.
- Dehydration (especially due to alcohol)

- Severe sunburn

- Overweight

- Lack of heat training

- Exercising more than one is used to

- Occurrence of heat disease in the past

- Two or more nights of extreme sleep deprivation

- Certain medical conditions including high cholesterol, high blood pressure, extreme stress, asthma, diabetes, epilepsy, cardiovascular disease, smoking, or a general lack of fitness

- Drug use, including alcohol, over-the-counter medications, prescription drugs, etc. (consult with your doctor about using drugs when you are exercising hard in hot weather).

TAKE ACTION! CALL 911.

Use your best judgment, but in most cases anyone who exhibits two or more of the symptoms should get into a cool environment, and get medical attention immediately. An extremely effective cool off method is to soak towels, sheets or clothing in cool or cold water, and wrap them around the individual. If ice is available, sprinkle some ice over the wet cloth.

CHAPTER 21

TROUBLESHOOTING PERFORMANCE

TIMES ARE SLOWING DOWN AT END

- Your long runs aren't long enough.
- You are running too fast at the beginning of the race.
- You may benefit from walk breaks that are taken more frequently or easing pace going uphill.
- You may be overtrained—back off the speed sessions for a week or two.
- In speed workouts, run faster at the end of the workout.
- Temperature and/or humidity may be to blame—try slowing down at the beginning.

SLOWING DOWN IN THE MIDDLE OF THE RACE

- You may be running too hard at the beginning—slow down during the first third of the race.

- In speed workouts, work faster in the middle of the workout.

NAUSEOUS AT THE END

- You ran too fast at the beginning.

- Temperature is above 65°F/17°C.

- You ate too much (or drank too much) before the race or workout—even hours before.

- You ate the wrong foods—most commonly, fat, fried foods, milk products, fibrous foods.

TIRED DURING WORKOUTS

- Low in B vitamins.

- Low in iron—have a serum ferritin test.

- Not eating enough protein.

- Blood sugar is low before exercise.

- Not eating a 200-300 calorie carbohydrate snack within 30 min of the finish of a previous run (to restock muscle glycogen).

- Eating too much fat—especially before or right after a run.

- Running too many days per week.

- Running too hard on long runs.

- Running too hard on all running days.

- Not taking enough walk breaks from the beginning of your long runs.

REASONS WHY YOU MAY NOT BE IMPROVING

1. You're overtrained and tired—if so, reduce your training, and/or take an extra rest day.

2. You may have chosen a goal that is too ambitious for your current ability.

3. You may have missed some of your workouts, or not been as regular with your training.

4. The temperature may have been above 60°F (15°C). Above this, you will slow down (the longer the race, the more effect heat will make on the result).

5. When using different courses, one of them may not have been accurately measured. This happens often in cross-country.

6. You ran the first half too fast.

CHAPTER 22

PROBLEMS AND SOLUTIONS

SIDE PAIN

This is very common, and usually has a simple fix. Normally it is nothing to worry about... it just hurts. This condition is due to 1) the lack of deep breathing, and 2) going a little too fast from the beginning of the run. You can correct #2 easily by walking more at the beginning, and/or slowing down your running pace during the first few minutes of running.

Deep breathing from the beginning of a run can prevent side pain. This way of inhaling air is performed by diverting the air you breathe into your lower lungs. Also called "belly breathing", this is how we breathe when asleep, and it provides maximum opportunity for oxygen absorption. If you don't deep breathe when you run, and you are not getting the oxygen you need, the side pain will tell you. By slowing down, walking, and breathing deeply for a while, the pain may go away. But sometimes it does not. Most runners just continue to run with the side pain. In 60 years of running and helping others run, I've not seen any lasting negative effect due to running with a side pain—it just hurts.

You don't have to take in a maximum breath to perform this technique. Simply breathe a normal breath but send it to the lower lungs. You know that you have done this if your stomach goes up and down as you inhale and exhale. If your chest goes up and down, you are breathing shallowly.

 NOTE: **Never breathe in and out rapidly. This can lead to hyperventilation, dizziness, and fainting.**

I FEEL GREAT ONE DAY... AND NOT THE NEXT

If you can solve this problem, you could become a very wealthy person. There are a few common reasons for this, but there will always be "those days" when the body doesn't seem to work right, or the gravity seems heavier than normal—and you cannot find a reason. You should keep looking for the causes of this in your journal. If you feel this way several times a week, for two or more weeks in a row, you may need more rest in your program.

1. Just do it. In most cases, this is a one-day occurrence. Most runners just put more walking into the mix, slow down, and get through it. Before doing a speed workout, however, make sure that there's not a medical reason for the "bad" feeling. I've had some of my best workouts after feeling very bad during the first few miles—or the first few speed repetitions.

2. Heat and/or humidity will make you feel worse. You will often feel better when the temperature is below 60°F and miserable when 75°F or above—and/or the humidity is high.

3. Low blood sugar can make any run a bad run. You may feel good at the start and suddenly feel like you have no energy. Every step seems to take a major effort.

4. Low motivation. Use the rehearsal techniques in chapter 27 to get you out the door on a bad day. These have helped numerous runners turn their minds around—even in the middle of a run.

5. Infection can leave you feeling lethargic, achy, and unable to run at the same pace that was easy a few days earlier. Check the normal signs (fever, chills, swollen lymph glands, higher morning pulse rate, etc.) and at least call your doctor if you suspect something.

6. Medication and alcohol, even when taken the day before, can leave a hangover that may not affect any area of your life except for your running. Your doctor or

pharmacist should be able to tell you about the effect of medication on strenuous exercise.

7. A slower start can make the difference between a good day and a bad day. When your body is on the edge of fatigue or other stress, it only takes a few seconds too fast per mile to push into discomfort or worse. A quick adjustment to a slightly slower pace before you get too tired can turn this around.

8. Caffeine can help because it gets the central nervous system working to top capacity. I feel better and my legs work so much better when I have had a cup of coffee an hour before the start of a run. Of course, those who have any problems with caffeine should avoid it—or consult a doctor.

UPSET STOMACH OR DIARRHEA

Sooner or later, virtually every runner has at least one episode with nausea or diarrhea. It comes from the buildup of total stress that you accumulate in your life— and specifically the stress of the workout. But stress is the result of many unique conditions within the individual. Your body produces the nausea/diarrhea (N/D) to get you to reduce the exercise, which will reduce the stress. Here are the common causes.

1. **Running too fast or too far** is the most common cause. Runners are confused about this, because the pace doesn't feel too fast in the beginning. Each person has a level of fatigue that triggers these conditions. Slowing down (especially during the first third of a race) and taking more walk breaks (on long runs) will help you manage the problem. Speed training and racing will increase stress very quickly.

2. **Eating too much or too soon before the run.** Your system has to work hard when running, and it is also hard work to digest food. Doing both at the same time raises stress and results in nausea, etc. Having food in your stomach, in the process of being digested is an extra stress and a likely target for elimination.

3. **Eating a high fat or high protein diet.** Even one meal that has over 50% of the calories in fat or protein can lead to N/D hours later—when you run.

4. **Eating too much the afternoon or evening the day before.** A big evening meal will still be in the gut the next morning, being digested. When you bounce up and down on a run, which you will, you add stress to the system, sometimes resulting in N/D.

5. **Heat and humidity** are a major cause of these problems. Some people don't adapt well to even modest heat increases and experience N/D when racing (or doing speed sessions) at the same pace that did not produce the problem in cool weather.

In hot conditions, everyone has a core body temperature increase that will result in significant stress to the system—often causing nausea, and sometimes diarrhea. By slowing down, taking more walk breaks, and pouring water over your head, you can manage this better. The best effect comes from slowing down from the beginning of a run on a hot day.

6. Drinking too much water before a run. If you have too much water in your stomach, and you are bouncing around, you put stress on the digestive system. Reduce your intake to the bare minimum. Most runners don't need to drink any fluid before a run that is 60 minutes or less.

7. Drinking too much of a sugar/electrolyte drink. Water is the easiest substance for the body to process. The addition of sugar and/or electrolyte minerals, as in a sports drink, makes the substance harder to digest. During a run (especially on a hot day) it is best to drink only water if you have had N/D or other problems. Cold water is best. But even too much water can upset the system.

8. Drinking too much fluid (especially a sugar drink) too soon after a run. Even if you are very thirsty, don't gulp down large quantities of any fluid during a short period of time. Try to drink no more than 6-8 oz, every 20 minutes or so. If you are particularly prone to N/D, just take 2-4 sips, every 5 minutes or so. When the body is very stressed and tired, it's not a good idea to consume a sugar drink (sports drink, etc). The extra stress of digesting the sugar can lead to problems.

9. Don't let running be stressful to you. Some runners get too obsessed about getting their run in or running at a specific pace. This adds stress to your life. Relax and let your run diffuse some of the other tensions in your life. Coaches can help in this area.

HEADACHE

There are several reasons why runners get headaches on runs. While uncommon, they happen to the average runner about 1-5 times a year. The extra stress that running puts on the body can trigger a headache on a tough day—even considering the relaxation that comes from the run. Many runners find that one dose of an over-the- counter headache medication takes care of the problem. As always, consult with your doctor about use of medication. Here are some of the causes/solutions.

Dehydration—if you run in the morning, make sure that you hydrate well the day before. Avoid alcohol if you run in the mornings and have headaches. Also watch the salt in your dinner meal the night before. A good sports drink like Accelerade, taken throughout the day the day before, will help to keep your fluid levels and your electrolytes "topped off." If you run in the afternoon, follow the same advice leading up to your run, on the day of the run. If you are dehydrated an hour before a run, it doesn't help to drink a huge amount of water at that time—6-8 oz is fine.

Medications can often produce dehydration—there are some medications that make runners more prone to headaches. Check with your doctor.

Too hot for you—run at a cooler time of the day (usually in the morning before the sun gets above the horizon). When on a hot run, pour water over your head.

Being in the sun—try to stay in the shade as much as possible. Wear a visor not a hat, making sure the band is not too tight.

Running a little too fast—start all runs more slowly, walk more during the first half of the run.

Running farther than you have run in the recent past—monitor your mileage and don't increase more than about 15% farther than you have run on any single run in the recent past. When increasing (or when running any long run) it helps to slow down more with each run, and take walk breaks more often.

Low blood sugar level—be sure that you boost your BSL with a snack, about 30-60 min before you run. If you are used to having it, caffeine in a beverage can sometimes help this situation also—but caffeine causes headaches for a small percentage of runners.

If prone to migraines—generally avoid caffeine, and try your best to avoid dehydration. Talk to your doctor about other possibilities.

Watch your neck and lower back—if you have a slight forward lean as you run, you can put pressure on the spine—particularly in the neck and lower back. Remember to run upright.

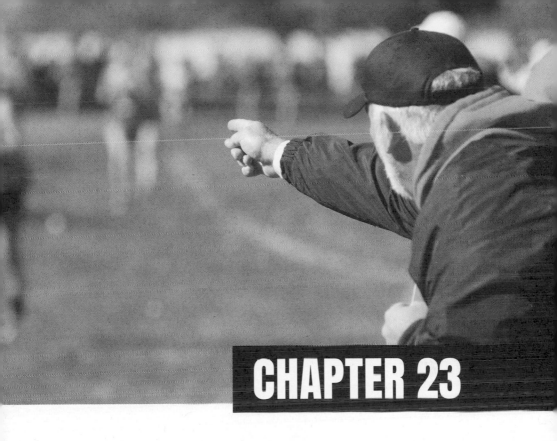

CHAPTER 23

INJURY TROUBLESHOOTING...
FROM ONE RUNNER TO ANOTHER

NOTE: As with all medical issues, ask a doctor who is supportive of your running.

QUICK TREATMENT TIPS

For all injuries:

1. Take 3 days off from running or any activity that could aggravate the area.

2. Avoid any activity that could aggravate the injury.

3. As you return to running, stay below the threshold of further irritation with much more liberal walking.

4. Don't stretch unless you have iliotibial band injury. Stretching interferes with the healing of most injuries.

MUSCLE INJURIES

1. Call your doctor's office and see if you can take prescription strength anti-inflammatory medication. Always follow your doctor's advice about medication.

2. See a sports massage therapist who has worked successfully on many runners.

TENDON AND FOOT INJURIES

1. Rub a chunk of ice directly on the area for 15 minutes every night (keep rubbing until the area gets numb—about 15 minutes).

2. Foot injuries sometimes are helped by an air cast at first to let the foot or leg to be stabilized so that the healing can begin.

KNEE INJURIES

1. Call your doctor's office to see if you can take prescription strength anti-inflammatory medication.

2. See if you can do a little gentle walking, sometimes this helps.

3. Sometimes the knee straps can relieve pain, ask your doctor.

4. Get a shoe check to see if you are in the right shoe (if you overpronate, a motion control shoe may help).

5. If you overpronate, an orthotic may help.

6. If you have internal knee pain, a glucosamine supplement may help.

SHIN INJURIES

1. Rule out a stress fracture. In this case, the pain usually gets worse as you run—but check with your doctor.

2. If the pain gradually goes away as you run on it, there is less worry of a stress fracture. This is probably a shin splint. If you stay below the threshold of activity that irritates the shin muscle, you can run with shin splints as they gradually go away (check with doctor to be sure).

3. Take more walk breaks, run more slowly, etc.

STARTING RUNNING BEFORE THE INJURY HAS HEALED

With most running injuries, you can continue to run even while the injury is healing. Always check with a doctor to be sure. But first, you must have some time off to get the healing started. If you do this at the beginning of an injury many runners only need 2-5 days off. The longer you try to push through the problem, the more damage you produce and the longer it will take to heal. Stay in touch with the doc at any stage of this healing/running process, follow his/her advice, and use your best judgment.

To allow for healing, once you have returned to running, stay below the threshold of further irritation. In other words, if the injury feels a little irritated when running at 2.5 miles, and starts hurting a little at 3 miles, you should run no more than 2 miles. And if your "healthy" run-walk ratio is 3 min run/1 min walk, you should drop back to 1-1 or 30 seconds/30 seconds.

Always allow a day of rest between running days. With most injuries you can cross-train to maintain conditioning, but make sure that your injury will allow this. Again, your doctor can advise.

BEST CROSS-TRAINING MODES TO MAINTAIN YOUR RUNNING CONDITIONING

Before doing any of these ask your doctor. Most are fine for most injuries. But some increase the risk of irritating the injured area and delaying the healing process. For more information on this, see chapter 17. Gradually build up the cross-training, because you have to condition these those muscles gradually as you do the ones in running. Even walking is a great way to maintain conditioning if the injury and the doctor will allow it.

1. Running in the water can improve your running form

2. Nordic Track machines

3. Walking

4. Rowing machines

5. Elliptical machines

There is much more information on specific injuries in my RUNNING INJURIES: CARE & TREATMENT and GALLOWAY'S BOOK ON RUNNING. But here are some helpful items that I want to pass on as one runner to another.

TREATMENT SUGGESTIONS—FROM ONE RUNNER TO ANOTHER

KNEE PAIN

Most knee problems will go away if you stop running immediately (don't run the last mile) and take 5 days off. Ask your doctor if you can use anti-inflammatory medication. Try to figure out what caused the knee problem. Make sure that your running courses don't have a slant or canter. Look at the most worn pair of shoes you have, even walking shoes. If there is wear on the inside of the forefoot, you probably overpronate. If you have repeat issues with knee pain, you may need a foot support or orthotic. If there is pain under the kneecap, or arthritis, the glucosamine/chondroitin products have helped.

OUTSIDE OF THE KNEE PAIN—ILIOTIBIAL BAND SYNDROME

This band of fascia acts as a tendon, going down the outside of the leg from the hip to just below the knee. The pain is most commonly noticed on the outside of the knee, but can occur anywhere along the IT band. I believe this to be a "wobble injury." When the running muscles get tired, they don't keep you on a straight running track. The IT band tries to restrain the wobbling motion, but it cannot and gets overused. Most of the feedback I receive from runners and doctors is that once the healing has started (usually a few days off from running), most runners will heal as fast when running on it as from a complete layoff. In this case, however it is crucial to get your doctor's OK to run, and then, to stay below the threshold of further irritation.

Treatment for the IT band:

1. Stretching: Stretching the IT band releases the tightness that produces the pain. With this injury you can stretch before, after, and even during a run.

2. Self-massage using a foam roller. This device has helped thousands of runners get over IT band issues. Put the roller on the floor, lie on it using body weight to press and roll the area that is sore. Rolling before a run will help it "warm up", and rolling afterward often helps the injury recover faster.

3. Massage Therapy: an experienced and accomplished massage therapist can tell whether massage will help and where to massage. The two areas for possible attention are the connecting points of the connective tissue that is tight, and the fascia band itself, in several places. "The stick" is a self massage roller device that has also helped many runners recover from IT band problems as they run. As with the foam roller, it helps to warm up the area before a run, and to roll it out afterward.

4. Walking is usually fine—and usually you can find a run-walk ratio that works. Maintain a short stride.

5. Direct ice massage on the area of pain: 15 minutes of continuous rubbing every night.

SHIN PAIN—"SHIN SPLINTS" OR STRESS FRACTURE

Almost always, pain in this area indicates a minor irritation called "shin splints" that allows running and walking as you heal. With normal shin splints, the greatest pain or irritation during injury is during the first mile of a run. Gradually the pain usually goes away as you run and walk. It takes a while to fully heal, so you must have patience.

*   Inside pain—posterior shin splints. Irritation of the inside of the leg, coming up from the ankle is called "posterior tibial shin splints" and is often due to overpronation of the foot (foot rolls in at push-off).

*   Front of shin—anterior shin splints. When the pain is in the muscle on the front of the lower leg it is "anterior tibial shin splints." This is very often due to having too long a stride when running and especially when walking. Downhill terrain should be avoided as much as possible during the healing process.

*   Stress fracture. If the pain is in a very specific place, and increases as you run, you could have a more serious problem: a stress fracture. This is unusual for beginning runners, but characteristic of those who do too much, too soon. It can also indicate low bone density. If you even suspect a stress fracture, do not run or do anything stressful on the leg and see a doctor. Stress fractures take weeks of no running and walking, usually wearing a cast. They may also indicate a calcium deficiency.

HEEL PAIN—PLANTAR FASCIA

The most effective treatment is putting your foot in a supportive shoe before your first step in the morning.

This very common injury (pain on the inside or center of the heel) is felt when you first walk on the foot in the morning. As you get warmed up, it gradually goes away, only to return the next morning. The most important treatment is to put your foot in a supportive shoe, before you step out of bed. Be sure to get a "shoe check" at a technical running store to make sure that you have the right shoe for your foot. If the pain continues during the day, you should consult with a podiatrist. Usually the doctor will construct a foot support that will surround your arch and heel. This does not always need to be a hard orthotic and is usually a softer one designed for your foot with support in the right places.

The "toe squincher" exercise noted in this book can help develop foot strength that will also support the foot. It takes several weeks for this to take effect. This is another injury that allows for running as you heal, but stay in touch with your doctor.

BACK OF THE FOOT—ACHILLES TENDON

The Achilles tendon is the narrow band of tendon rising up from the heel and connecting to the calf muscle. It is part of a very efficient mechanical system, which performs like a strong rubber band to leverage a lot of work out of the foot, with a little effort from the calf muscle. It is usually injured due to excessive stretching, either through running or through stretching exercises. First, avoid any activity that stretches the tendon in any way. It helps to add a small heel lift to all shoes, which reduces the range of motion. Every night, rub a chunk of ice directly on the tendon. Keep rubbing for about 15 minutes, until the tendon gets numb. Bags of ice or frozen gels don't do any good at all in my opinion. Usually after 3-5 days off from running, the icing takes hold and the Achilles feels stronger each day. Anti-inflammatory medication very rarely helps with the Achilles tendon, in my experience.

HIP AND GROIN PAIN

There are a variety of elements that could be aggravated in the hip area. Since the hips are not designed to move you down the road, they are usually abused when you continue to push on, when the calf muscle is too tired to keep you going at top capacity. Ask your doctor about prescription strength anti-inflammatory medication, as this can sometimes speed up recovery. Avoid stretching and any activity that aggravates the area.

CALF MUSCLE

The calf is the most important muscle for running. It is often irritated by speedwork, and can be pushed into injury by stretching, running too fast when tired, by too many speed sessions without adequate rest between, and sprinting at the end of races or workouts.

Deep tissue massage has been the best treatment I've found for most calf muscle problems. Try to find a very experienced massage therapist who has helped lots of runners with calf problems. This can be painful but may be the only way to remove some bio-damage in the muscle. The "stick" can be very beneficial in manipulating tissue out of the area of damage—and promoting blood flow (see our website for more information on this product).

Don't stretch! Stretching will tear the muscle fibers that are trying to heal. Avoid running hills, and take very frequent walk breaks as you return to running. A slight heel lift (felt, etc.) can take pressure off the Achilles and calf muscles to reduce aggravation. As the pain goes away, remove the heel pad.

CHOOSING THE BEST SHOE FOR YOU

The best advice I can give you... is to get the best advice. If you have a good technical running store in your area, go there. The advice you can receive from experienced shoe fitters is priceless. Here are some other helpful tips:

1. Look at the wear pattern on your most worn pair of walking or running shoes. Use the guide below to help you choose about 3 pairs of shoes from one of the following categories:

- Floppy feet have spots of wear, including some wear on the inside of the forefoot.

- If you have spots of wear, and have some foot or knee pain, select a shoe that has minimal cushion, or is designed for motion control.

OVERPRONATED FOOT?

This wear pattern shows significant wear on the inside of the forefoot. If there is knee or hip pain, look for a shoe that has "structure" or motion-control capabilities. If you don't have pain, look at a neutral shoe that does not have a lot of cushion in the forefoot.

RIGID?

If you have a wear pattern on the outside of the forefoot of the shoe, and no wear on the inside, you probably have a rigid foot, and can choose a neutral shoe that has adequate cushion and flexibility for you, as you run and walk in them.

CAN'T TELL?

1. Choose shoes that are neutral or have a mid range of cushion and support.

2. Set aside at least 30 minutes to choose your next shoe, so that you can compare the 3 candidates you have chosen.

3. Run and walk on a pavement surface to compare the shoes. If you have a floppy or overpronated foot, make sure that you get the support you need.

4. You want a shoe that feels natural—no pressure or aggravation—while allowing the foot to go through the range of motion needed for running. Runners that need motion control should feel reasonably secure in the shoe.

5. Take as much time as you need before deciding

6. If the store doesn't let you run in the shoe, go to another store

Don't worry about the size on the box—go for the fit. Most runners wear a running shoe that is about 2 sizes larger than their street shoe. For example, I wear a size 10 street shoe but run in a size 12 running model.

Leave about half to three-quarters of an inch of extra toe room. Your foot tends to swell during the day, so it's best to fit your shoes after noontime. Be sure to stand up in the shoe during the fitting process to measure how much extra room you have in the toe region of the shoe. Pay attention to the longest part of your feet, and leave at least half an inch.

WIDTH ISSUES

*   Running shoes tend to be a bit wider than street shoes.

*   Usually, the lacing can "snug up" the difference, if your foot is a bit narrower.

*   The shoe shouldn't be laced too tight around your foot because the foot swells during running and walking. On hot days, the average runner will move up one- half shoe size.

*   In general, running shoes are designed to handle a certain amount of "looseness." But if you are getting blisters when wearing a loose shoe, tighten the laces.

- Some shoe companies have some models that come in various widths.

- The shoe is too narrow if you are rolling off the edge of the shoe as you push off— on either side.

SHOES FOR WOMEN

Women's shoes tend to be slightly narrower than those for men, and the heel is usually a bit smaller. About 25% of women runners have feet that can fit better into men's shoes— usually in the larger sizes. The better running stores can help you make a choice in this area.

BREAKING IN A NEW SHOE

- Wear the new shoe around the house for an hour or more each day for a week. If you stay on carpet, and the shoe doesn't fit correctly, you can exchange it at the store. But if you have put some wear on the shoe, dirt, etc., few stores will take it back

- In most cases runners find that shoes are comfortable enough to run in then immediately. It is best, however, to continue walking in the shoe, gradually allowing the foot to accommodate to the arch, the heel, the ankle pads, and to make other adjustments. If you run in the shoe too soon, blisters are often the result.

- If there are no rubbing issues on the foot when walking, you could walk in the new shoe for a gradually increasing amount for 2-4 days.

- At that point, run about half a mile in the shoe. Put on your old shoes and continue the run.

- On each successive run, increase the distance run in the new shoe for 3-4 runs. At this point, you will usually have the new shoe broken in.

HOW DO YOU KNOW WHEN IT'S TIME TO GET A NEW SHOE?

1. When you have been using a shoe for 3-4 weeks successfully, buy another pair of exactly the same model, make, size, etc. The reason for this: The shoe companies often make significant changes or discontinue shoe models (even successful ones) every 6-8 months.

2. Walk around the house in the new shoe for a few days.

3. After the shoe feels broken in, run the first half mile of one of your weekly runs (shoe break-in day) in the new shoe, then put on the shoe that is already broken in.

4. On this weekly shoe comparison, gradually run a little more in the new shoe.

5. Several weeks later you will notice that the new shoe offers more bounce than the old one.

6. When the old shoe doesn't offer the support you need, shift to the new pair.

7. Start breaking in a third pair.

THE CLOTHING THERMOMETER

After years of coaching runners in various climates, here are my recommendations for the appropriate clothing based upon the temperature. The first layer, since it will be next to your skin, should feel comfortable, and designed to move the moisture away from your skin. You may have to resist the temptation to buy a fashion color, but function is most important. As you try on the clothing in the store watch for seams and extra material in areas where you will have body parts rubbing together, thousands of times during a run.

Cotton is usually not a good fabric for those who perspire a great deal. The cotton will absorb the sweat, hold it next to your skin, and increase the weight you must carry during the run. Garments made out of fabric labeled Polypro, Coolmax, Drifit, etc., can retain enough body heat to keep you warm in winter, while releasing the extra amount. By moving moisture to the outside of the garment, you will stay cooler in summer, while avoiding the winter chill.

Temperature	What to Wear
14°C or 60°F and above	Tank top or singlet, and shorts
9 to 13°C or 50 to 59°F	T-shirt and shorts
5 to 8°C or 40 to 49°F	Long-sleeve lightweight shirt, shorts or tights (or nylon long pants), mittens or gloves
0 to 4°C or 30 to 39°F	Medium-weight long-sleeve shirt, and another T shirt, tights and shorts, socks, mittens or gloves and a hat over the ears
-4 to -1°C or 20-29°F	Medium-weight long-sleeve shirt, another T-shirt, tights and shorts, socks, mittens or gloves, and a hat over the ears
-4 to -1°C or 20-29°F	Medium-weight long-sleeve shirt, another T-shirt, tights and shorts, socks, mittens or gloves, and a hat over the ears
-8 to -3C or 10-19F	Medium-weight long-sleeve shirt, and medium/heavy weight shirt, tights and shorts, nylon wind suit, top and pants, socks, thick mittens and a hat over the ears
-12 to -7C or 0-9F	Two medium- or heavy-weight long-sleeve tops, thick tights, thick underwear (especially for men), medium to heavy warm-up suit, gloves and thick mittens, ski mask, a hat over the ears, and Vaseline covering any exposed skin.
-18 to -11C or -15F	Two heavy-weight long-sleeve tops, thick tights, thick underwear (and supporter for men), thick warm-up suit (top and pants), mittens over gloves, thick ski mask and a hat over ears, Vaseline covering any exposed skin, thicker socks on your feet and other foot protection, as needed.
-20 both C & F	Add layers as needed

WHAT NOT TO WEAR

1. A heavy coat in winter. If the layer is too thick, you'll heat up, sweat excessively, and cool too much when you take it off.

2. No shirt for men in summer. Fabric that holds some of the moisture will give you more of a cooling effect as you run and walk.

3. Socks that are too thick in summer. Your feet swell and the pressure from the socks can increase the chance of a black toenail and blisters.

4. Lime green shirt with bright pink polka dots (unless you have a lot of confidence and/or can run fast).

Special cases:

Chaffing can be reduced by lycra and other fabric. Many runners have eliminated chaffing between the legs by using a lycra "bike tight" as an undergarment. These are also called "lycra shorts." There are also several skin lubricants on the market, including Glide.

Some men suffer from irritation of their nipples. Having a slick and smooth fabric across the chest will reduce this.

PRACTICAL EATING ISSUES

Most of the nutritional problems that I hear about are due to eating too much or too soon before running. In a minority of cases, nutritional problems are the result of low blood sugar or consuming the wrong foods. While there are many individual differences in all of the eating variables, it's always better to err on the side of eating less as it gets closer to the workout or race.

Practical eating issues

- You don't need to eat before a run, unless your blood sugar is low.

- Reload most effectively by eating approximately 200 calories within 30 min of the finish of a run (80% carb/20% protein). Avoid fat within 60 minutes of the finish of a hard run.

- Eating or drinking too much right before the start of a run will interfere with deep breathing, and may cause side pain. The food or fluid in your stomach limits your intake of air into the lower lungs, and restricts the diaphragm—causing pain in the area just below the ribs.

- If you are running low on blood sugar at the end of your long runs or long workouts, take some blood sugar booster with you (gels, gummy bears, etc.)

- It is never a good idea to eat a huge meal. Those who claim that they must "carbo load" are often rationalizing the desire to eat a lot of food. Eating a big meal the night before (or the day of) a race, or before a hard workout or a long run—can be a real problem. The food will require an extensive blood flow to the gut, depriving the exercising muscles of this precious fluid. In addition, you will have a lot of food in your gut, as you bounce up and down during your race. The results could be ugly.

A radical change in the foods you eat, is not a good idea, and usually leads to problems—especially within 12 hours before a hard workout or race. Before long runs and hard workouts, fine-tune your eating schedule and replicate the routine that works for you leading up to your races.

SWEAT THE ELECTROLYTES

Electrolytes are the salts that your body loses when you sweat: sodium, potassium, magnesium and calcium. You cannot replace these during long runs because your absorption system shuts down under the stress of the run. When you have not restocked your supply of these, through eating and drinking the day after a hard workout, your fluid transfer system doesn't work as well and you may experience ineffective cooling, muscle cramps, and other problems.

Most runners have no problem replacing these in a normal diet, but if you are regularly experiencing cramping during or after exercise, you may be low in sodium or potassium. The best product I've found for replacing these minerals is called SUCCEED. If you have high blood pressure, a mineral imbalance, etc., get your doctor's guidance before taking any salt supplement.

When you are sweating a lot, it is a good idea to drink several glasses a day of a good electrolyte beverage.

DRINKING/EATING SCHEDULE BEFORE A HARD MORNING RUN

- 1-2 hours before a morning run: either a cup of coffee, diet drink or a glass of water. If you need to eat something, have half of an energy bar or a packet of a gel-type product.

- 30 min before any run (if blood sugar is low and you have not had any food) approximately 100 calories of a drink that has 80% carbohydrate and 20% protein (Accelerade, for example).

- Within 30 min after a run: approximately 200 calories of an 80% carb/20% protein (Endurox R4, for example).

- If you are sweating a lot during hot weather, 3-4 glasses of a good electrolyte beverage like Accelerade, throughout the day.

GET INSULIN WORKING FOR YOU

For best results in raising blood sugar when it is too low (within 30 minutes before a run) a snack should have about 80% of the calories in simple carbohydrate and 20% in protein. This promotes the production of insulin which is helpful before a run in processing the carbohydrate into a form (glycogen) that the muscles can use very quickly. The product Accelerade has worked best among the thousands of runners I hear from every year. It has the 80/20 ratio of carbohydrate to protein. If you eat an energy bar with the 80/20 ratio, be sure to drink 6-8 oz of water or coffee with it. Many runners consume an energy bar (or half an energy bar) about an hour before exercise.

EATING DURING EXERCISE

Most exercisers don't need to worry about eating or drinking during a run. In fact, the body shuts down in its ability to process almost anything, and eating even sports nutrition products can make you nauseous. But when your slow long runs exceed 90 minutes, the blood sugar level starts to drop. At this point, there are several options listed here. Most runners find it productive to start taking the food product about 50-60 minutes into the workout. This helps when running long, or during a long session of speed segments.

Gel-type products—these come in small packets, and are the consistency of honey or thick syrup. The most successful way to take them is to put the contents of 1-2 packets in a small plastic bottle with a pop-top. About every 10-15 minutes, take a small squirt with a sip or two of water.

Energy bars—Cut into 8-10 pieces and take a piece, with a couple of sips of water, every 10-15 minutes.

Candy—particularly gummy bears or hard candies. The usual consumption is 1-2 pieces, about every 10 minutes.

Sports drinks—Since nausea is experienced by a significant number of those who drink these products during exercise, I'm not going to recommend this. If you have had success, when using sports drinks in workouts or races, drink it in the same quantity and on the same schedule as you have used before. Water is the fluid that is used most successfully by the athletes I've worked with over the years.

Exception: During your rest interval, when doing prolonged workouts of speed repetitions, a slightly diluted sports drink like Accelerade has helped maintain BSL and reduced recovery time, according to research.

IT IS IMPORTANT TO RELOAD WITHIN 30 MINUTES AFTER EXERCISE

Whenever you have finished a hard or long workout (for you), a reloading snack of about 200-300 calories will help you recover faster. Again, the 80/20 ratio of carb to protein has been most successful in replenishing the glycogen stores into the muscle cells. The recovery product that has worked best for the thousands of runners I work with each year is Endurox R4.

CHAPTER 26

THE FINAL COUNTDOWN BEFORE A RACE

THE AFTERNOON BEFORE

Some like to run a little and some don't run the day before the race. You won't lose any conditioning if you take two days off from running leading up to the race. This is a personal or team issue and the number of days you do not run before a race is your choice. Most coaches prefer that their athletes run together, on one of these days, to consolidate team spirit.

THE CARBO LOADING DINNER

Some teams have a dinner the night before. At the dinner you can talk strategy, and enjoy the evening. Don't over-eat! Many runners assume, mistakenly, that they must eat a lot of food the night before. This is actually counterproductive. It takes at least 36 hours for most of the food you eat to be processed and useable in a race—usually longer. It is very unlikely that you will get any significant nutritional help from the "last supper" before the race.

A lot of food in your gut, when you are bouncing up and down in a race, is stressful. A very common and embarrassing situation occurs when the gut is emptied to relieve this stress. While you don't want to starve yourself the afternoon and evening before, the best strategy is to eat small meals or snacks that you know are easy for the body to digest, and taper down the amount as you get closer to bed time. As always, it's best to have done a "rehearsal" of eating, so that you know what works, how much, when to stop eating, and what foods to avoid. Work on your eating plan the evening before each race, come up with a successful menu, and replicate as you approach raceday.

DRINKING

The day before, drink 8 glasses of fluid, spread throughout the day, with two of them being a sports drink. Don't drink a lot of fluid during the morning of the race itself. This can lead to bathroom breaks before the race or the desire to do so during the race itself. Many races have porto-johns around the start area, but some do not. This is another reason to preview the venue—and note the locations of bathrooms. The best solution for most runners is to drink 6-8 oz of fluid about 2-3 hours before the race. In most cases, this is out of the system before the start.

> **DRINKING TIP:** If you practice drinking before each race, you can find the right amount of fluid that works best for you—as the season progresses. Stage your drinks so that you know when you will be taking potty breaks, comfortably before the start of the race itself.

THE NIGHT BEFORE

For those who have had digestive problems during other races, eating is optional after 5pm. If you are hungry, have a light snack (or two) that you have tested before, and has not caused problems. Less is better, but don't go to bed hungry. Continue to have about 8oz of a good electrolyte beverage like Accelerade, within the 3 hours before you go to bed.

Alcohol is not recommended for any young athlete. Drinking alcohol the night before competition can reduce performance potential. The effects of this central nervous system depressant carry over to the next morning. Alcohol is also a dehydrating agent.

PACKING LIST

Pack your bag and lay out your clothes so that you don't have to think very much on race morning.

- Your watch

- A pace chart, or wrist band, with split times, or mile times

- Shoes

- Socks

- Shorts

- Top—see clothing thermometer

- Outer garment in case of precipitation. Many use a garbage bag, with a "head hole"

- Pin race number on the front of the garment in which you will be finishing

- Bring along a few extra safety pins for your race number, or bib number

- Water, Accelerade, pre-race and post-race beverages (such as Endurox R4), and a cooler if you wish

- Food for the drive home

- Bandages, skin lubricant, any other first aid items you may need

- Cash for post-race celebration meal

- A few inspirational thoughts, jokes or stories to provide laughs or entertainment before the start

- Team garments, etc.

SLEEP

You may sleep well, or you may not. Don't worry about it if you don't sleep at all. Many runners I work with every year don't sleep at all the night before and have the best race of their lives. Of course, don't try to go sleepless... but if it happens, don't worry about it.

RACE DAY CHECKLIST

Photocopy this list so that you will not only have a plan, you can carry it out in a methodical way. Pack the list in your race bag. Don't try anything new the day of your race—except for health or safety issues. Stick with your successful plan.

Fluid and potty stops—after you wake up, drink 6-8 oz of water, 2-3 hours before the start (or use the plan that has worked for you). In order to avoid the bathroom stops, stop your fluid intake according to the timetable of what has worked for you before.

Eat—what you have eaten before your harder runs. Don't try anything new and avoid problem foods. It is OK not to eat at all before a race (5K or less) unless you have specific issues (such as diabetes), then go with the plan that you and your doctor have worked out.

Get your bearings—walk around the site to find where you want to line up, and how you will get to the start. Talk over strategy with teammates again.

Start your warm-up 40-50 min before the start. If possible, go backwards on the course and preview the start and finish segments for about half a mile each and turn around. This will give you a preview of the most important parts of your race—start and finish. Use the warm-up ritual that has worked for you in past workouts and races. Here is a standard one:

- Walk for 1-2 minutes, slowly.

- Jog slowly for 10 minutes.

- Over the next 15-18 minutes, jog over the start and the finish areas. Visualize starting and finishing.

- Walk around for 3-4 minutes.

- Do 4-8 acceleration-gliders that gradually get you up to the speed you will be running in the race.

- Talk strategy with teammates.

- Get in position and focus on your strategy for the first 200 yards.

- When runners are called to the start, stay with the team members you will be running with. Visualize how you are going to start the race—strong 200 meters (but not all out, then settling down to save energy for the rest of the first half. Think about passing runners during the second half of the race.

AFTER THE START

Remember that you can control how you feel during the last 400 meters by pacing and teamwork.

- After the first 200 yards, don't let yourself be pulled out too fast—run your pace.

- Stay with your plan. Keep key teammates in sight, and adjust. Don't spend resources in quick bursts—ease up and gradually increase the effort during the second half.

- Believe in yourself, say "This is my proven strategy for a strong finish."

- Even if you are pushing fairly hard, enjoy the race as much as possible, smile often.

- On warm days, pour water over your head at the start, possibly wetting your running top.

AFTER MID-RACE

- When the going gets tough, do everything you can to relax, and keep the muscles resilient.

- Keep going—don't give up. Shorten stride and pick up turnover—especially going uphill.

- During the last half-mile don't let your legs slow down. One more step! Success is not letting up. You can do it!

AT THE FINISH

- Your finish is important—you are running for the team.

- Keep a quick rhythm—even when very tired.

- Stay in the upright position.

- Cross the finish with a smile on your face.

- You did it!

AFTER THE FINISH

- Keep walking for at least a quarter of a mile.

- Drink about 4-8 oz of fluid.

- Within 30 min of the finish, have a snack that is 80% carbohydrate/20% protein (Endurox R4 is best).

- If you can soak your legs in cool water, during the first two hours after the race, do so (cool water faucet—ice is not necessary).

- Walk or jog for 20-30 minutes later in the day.

- Celebrate with team members!

THE NEXT DAY

- Walk for 30-60 minutes, very easy. This can be done at one time, or in installments.

- Keep drinking about 4-6 oz an hour of water or sports drink like Accelerade.

- Write down what you would do differently in your next race.

CHAPTER 27

MENTAL TOUGHNESS

You can gain control over your attitude through mental training.

The choice is yours. You can take control over your attitude, or you can let outside factors take you on a motivational roller coaster: fired up one day, and down the next. Whether you struggle to get out the door when running by yourself, or you need more motivation to keep going when it's tough in a race, you have a better chance of success when you have a strategy. This is your motivational training program.

To understand motivation, look inside the brain. Among the various circuits, are one that will bother you (left circuit) and one that will give you strength and solve problems (right circuit). The left or logical system does our business activities, trying to steer us into pleasure and away from discomfort. The creative and intuitive right circuit has access to an unlimited source of solutions to problems and connects us to hidden strengths.

As we accumulate stress, the left brain sends us a stream of messages telling us to "slow down," "stop and you'll feel better," "this isn't your day" and even philosophical messages like, "why are you doing this?" We are all capable of staying on track, and even pushing to a higher level of performance—even when the left brain is saying these things. So the first step in taking command over motivation is to ignore the left brain unless there is a legitimate reason of health or safety (very rare), or the reality that you are running a lot faster than you are ready to run in the race. You can deal with the left brain, through a series of mental training drills.

These drills allow the right side of the brain to keep searching for solutions to current problems, and empowerment. As the negative messages spew out of the left brain, the right brain doesn't argue. By preparing mentally for the challenges you expect, you will empower the right brain to deal with the problems and to develop mental toughness. Under right brain activity, the body tends to get the job done. You can empower the right brain by using three mental training strategies.

DRILL 1

REHEARSING SUCCESS

Getting out the door early in the morning

The most common motivational problem, as presented to me by cross-country runners, is how to get out of bed early enough, and be ready to do a hard workout or race well.

State your desired outcome: To be awake and fully engaged in the run, from the start.

Detail the challenge: Desire to lie in bed, no desire to exert yourself so early. The stress of the alarm clock, and having to think about what to do next when the brain isn't working very fast.

Break up the challenge into a series of actions, which lead you through the mental barriers, no one of which is challenging to the left brain.

1. The night before, lay out your running clothes and shoes (often near the coffee machine), so that you don't have to think.

2. Set your alarm, and say to yourself over and over: ALARM OFF... FEET ON FLOOR... TO THE KITCHEN. Or, simply stated:

    ALARM... FEET... KITCHEN

    As you repeat this, you visualize doing each action without thinking. By repeating it, you lull yourself to sleep. You have also been programming yourself to take action the next morning.

3. The alarm goes off. You shut it off, put feet on the floor, and you head to the kitchen—all without thinking.

4. You're putting on one piece of clothing at a time, sipping coffee (tea, diet cola, etc.), never thinking about exercise.

5. With coffee cup in hand, clothes on, and gear bag in hand, you stick your head out the door to see what the weather is like.

6. Driving to the workout or race, sipping your beverage, you rehearse seeing teammates, easing into the workout/race, feeling good about your exertion.

7. The endorphins are kicking in, you feel good, you want to continue.

Rehearsals develop patterns of thinking that get you in the groove to do the behaviors you need to do. In a challenging situation, you don't want to have to think about the stress or the challenge—you should take action: Move from one behavior to the next. The power of the rehearsal is that you have formatted your brain for a series of actions so that you don't have to think—and the sequence becomes almost automatic. By repeating the pattern, you'll revise it for real life, and become the successful runner you want to be!

Pushing past the fatigue point where you tend to slow down

You're into a hard workout or race, and you are really tired. Your left brain is telling you that you can't reach your goal today, "just slow down a little, there are other days to work hard."

Evaluate whether there is a real medical reason why you can't run as projected. If there is a reason, back off and conserve—there will be another day.

Almost every time, however, the problem is more simple: you are not willing to push through the discomfort. The most effective way of getting tough mentally is to gradually push back your limits. Speed training programs can help you greatly. As you add to the number of repetitions, each week, you'll work on the mind as the body gets all systems working together to run faster.

Confront left brain messages with strength statements: **Don't quit! I can do it!**

Mental toughness starts with, simply, not giving up. Just ignore the negative messages, and stay focused on the next few steps, continuously. Champions feel the same discomfort, they just hang on longer and get through it.

In your speed workouts, practice the following drill. Fine-tune this so that when you run your goal race, you will have a strategy for staying mentally tough.

The scene:

You're getting very tired, you'd really like to call it quits, or at least slow down significantly.

Quick strategies:

Break up the remaining workout or race into segments that you know you can do:

- "1 more minute"—Run for one minute, then reduce pace slightly for a few seconds, then say "1 more minute" again, and again.

- "10 more steps"—Run about 10 steps, take a couple of easy steps, then say "ten more steps."

- "One more step"—Keep saying this over and over—you'll get there.

Take some gliding breaks:

- Reduce the tension on your leg muscles and feet by gliding for a few strides every 1-2 minutes. The acceleration-glider drill prepares you for this moment, particularly when coasting downhill. This is particularly helpful when going uphill.

Segment by segment:

- In the workouts, if you really question your ability to get through the workout, start each repetition, or race segment, saying to your self—"just one more" (even if you have 4 to go) or "10 more steps." You'll make it the whole way.

- Teamwork! You are needed by the team. The belonging to a larger group, with team spirit can pull you through many difficult workouts or races.

- When you are getting close to the end and really feel like you can't keep going, say to yourself "I am tough" or "I can endure" or "Yes I can" or "One more step."

DRILL 2

MAGIC WORDS

Even the most motivated person has sections during a tough workout or race when he or she wants to quit. By using a successful brainwashing technique, you can pull yourself through these negative thoughts, and feel like a champion at the end. Associate these successes with key words and you can build on this success and confidence with each use.

Think back to the problems that you face in your tough workouts or races. These are the ones that are most likely to challenge you again. As you go through a series of speed sessions and long runs, you will confront just about every problem you will face. Go back in your memory bank and pull out instances when you started to lose motivation due to these, but finished and overcame the challenge.

Relax... Power... Glide

In really tough runs, I have three challenges that occur over and over: 1) I become tense when I get really tired, worried that I will struggle badly at the end. 2) I feel the loss of the bounce and strength I had at the beginning, and worry that there will be no strength at the end. 3) My form starts to get ragged and I worry about further deterioration of muscles and tendons and more fatigue due to "wobbling."

My big motivational breakthrough was learning to counter these three problems with the magic words "Relax... Power... Glide." The visualization of each of these positives helps a little. The real magic comes from the association I have made with hundreds of successful experiences when I started to "lose it" in one of the three areas, but overcame the problems. Each time I "run through" one or more of the challenges, I associate the experience with these magic words and add to the magic.

Now, when something starts to go wrong, I repeat the three words, over and over. Instead of increasing my anxiety, the repetition of the words calms me down. Even though I don't feel as strong in the last mile as I did in the first one, I'm empowered just by knowing that I have a strategy and can draw upon my past experience. And when my legs lose the efficient path and bounce, the right brain can take over and make adjustments as it has in past successes.

When I say magic words that are associated with successful experience, there are two positive effects. The saying of the words floods the brain with positive memories. For a while, the negative messages of the left brain don't have a chance and you can get down the course for a hundred yards or more. But the second effect may be more powerful. The words directly link you to the right brain, which works intuitively to make the same connections that allowed you solve the problems before.

To be successful on any day, you first need to finish the race. Most of the time you can get through the "bad parts" by not giving up, and simply putting one foot in front of the other. As you push beyond the negative left brain messages you create the confidence to do this again, and again. Feel free to use my magic words, or develop your own. The more experiences you have associated with the words, the more magic they have.

DRILL 3

DIRTY TRICKS

The strategy of the rehearsal drill will get you focused, organized, while reducing the stress for the first third to half of the race or workout. Magic words will pull you along through most of the remaining challenging sessions. But on the really rough days, it helps to have some dirty tricks to play on the left side of the brain.

These are quick fixes that distract the logical messages for a while, allowing you to keep going for the next segment of the course. These imaginative and sometimes crazy images don't have to have any logic behind them. But when you counter a left brain message with a creative idea, you can confuse the left brain and stop the flow of negative messages.

The giant invisible rubber band

When I get tired at the end of a hard race, I unpack this secret weapon, and throw it around someone ahead of me—or someone who had the audacity to pass me. For a while, the person doesn't realize that he or she has been "looped" and continues to push onward while I get the benefit of being pulled along. After a minute or two of mentally projecting myself into this image, I have to laugh for believing in such an absurd notion. But laughing activates the creative/resourceful right side of the brain. This usually generates several more entertaining ideas, especially when you do this on a regular basis.

The right brain has millions of dirty and entertaining tricks. Once you get it activated, you are likely to receive intuitive solutions to problems you are currently having. It can entertain you as you get closer to your finish, step-by-step. Most important, this circuit can empower the legs, feet, muscles to do what they are capable of doing on that day. The result will often surprise you.

For many more dirty tricks and mental strategies, see GALLOWAY'S BOOK ON RUNNING.

CHAPTER 28

PRODUCTS THAT ENHANCE RUNNING

For more information on these, visit www.JeffGalloway.com

Jeff Galloway Run Walk Run App

This app is designed to make the perfect custom plan for you, but one great part of this app is that you'll always be in control. You can adjust your pace and run-walk-run at any time, and the app's plan adjusts to match your needs. Also available are healthy meal plans to power your workouts, but you can customize them to match your preferences and dietary needs. I am your coach, but you're the captain of your own ship. Listen to me, but be sure to listen to your body as well so the plan can be adjusted as needed. Let's work together to get you across the finish line with a smile on your face. Available from the App Store and Google Play.

Other Galloway Books: training schedules, and gifts that keep on giving—even to yourself

(Order them, autographed, from *www.JeffGalloway.com*.)

Galloway's Marathon FAQ

There are over 100 of the most common questions I receive about marathon training and racing. You don't have to wade through pages of text to get the answers to your questions.

Running Injuries

I wrote this book with one of the most knowledgeable sports medicine experts I have met: David Hannaford, DPM. Each injury site is explained with suggestions for treatment. Also included are prevention strategies that have allowed me to run for over 30 years without an overuse injury.

Running—Testing Yourself

Training programs for 1 mile, 2 mile, 5K, and 1.5 mile are detailed, along with information on racing-specific information in nutrition, mental toughness, running form. There are also some very accurate prediction tests that allow you to tell what is a realistic goal. This book has been used effectively by those who are stuck in a performance rut at 10K or longer events. By training and racing faster, you can improve running efficiency and your tolerance for waste products, like lactic acid.

Running Until You're 100

In the chapter on joint health, you'll see in the research studies that runners have healthier joints than sedentary folks. In the chapter on the researched health benefits of exercise, an expert on longevity says that for every hour we exercise we can expect to get back 2 hours of life extension. Among the heroes section is an 85 year old who recently finished his 700th marathon. There are nutrition suggestions from Nancy Clark, training adjustments by decade, and many other helpful hints for running past the century mark.

Women's Complete Guide to Running and Women's Complete Guide to Walking

By Barbara and Jeff Galloway. The section on woman-specific issues makes this book unique: pregnancy, menstrual issues, bra fitting, incontinence, osteoporosis, inner organs shifting, menopause and more. There's a section for the unique problems of the "fabulously full figured" runners. Nutrition, fat burning, motivation, starting up, aches and pains—all are covered in the book. There's also a section in each book written by famous sports nutritionist Nancy Clark.

Running and Fat Burning for Women

By Barbara and Jeff Galloway. I've not seen another book that better describes the fat burning and accumulation process—with a strategy to take action. There are several important and inexpensive tools mentioned, with recipes, and specific suggestions about managing the calorie income and expenditure. There is also a section on women-specific issues.

Walking—The Complete Book

Walkers now have a book that explains the many benefits, how to maximize them, with training programs for 5K, 10K, Half and Full Marathons. There is resource information on fat burning, nutrition, motivation and much more.

Running—Getting Started

This is more than a state-of-the-art book for beginners. It gently takes walkers into running, with a 6-month schedule that has been very successful. Also included is information on fat-burning, nutrition, motivation, and body management. This is a great gift for your friends or relatives who can be "infected" positively by running.

Running—A Year-Round

Plan You'll find daily workouts for 52 weeks, for three levels of runners: to finish, to maximize potential, and time improvement. It has the long runs, speed sessions, drills, hill sessions, all listed, in the order needed to do a 5K, 10K, half marathon and marathonduring one year. Resource material is included to help with many running issues.

Galloway's Book on Running

This is the best-seller among running books since 1984. Thoroughly revised and expanded, you'll find training programs for 5K, 10K, half marathon, with nutrition, fat-burning, walk breaks, motivation, injuries, shoes, and much more. This is a total resource book.

Galloway's Half Marathon Training

This new edition provides highly successful and detailed training schedules for various time goals, for this important running goal. Information is provided on nutrition, mental preparation, fluids, race day logistics and checklist and much more.

Galloway's 5K/10K Running

Whether you want to finish with a smile on your face, or have a challenging time goal in mind, this book is a total resource for these distances. There are schedules for a wide range of performances, how to eat, how to predict your performance, how long and how fast to run on long runs, drills to improve form and speed training. There is extensive information on mental preparation, breaking through barriers, practical nutrition and more. The newest edition was released in 2021.

Your Personal Training Journal

Some type of journal is recommended to organize, and track, your training plan. It can be ordered from *www.JeffGalloway.com*, autographed. It simplifies the process, with places to fill in information for each day. There is also space for recording the unexpected thoughts and experiences that make so many runs come alive again as we read them.

Running Schools and Retreats:

Jeff conducts motivating running schools and retreats. These feature individualized information, form evaluation, comprehensively covering running, nutrition, and fat burning.

The Stick

This massage tool can help the muscles recover quicker. It will often speed up the recovery of muscle injuries or Iliotibial Band injuries (on the outside of the upper leg, between knee and hip). This type of device can warm up the leg muscles and reduce the aggravation of sore muscles and tendons. By promoting blood flow during and after a massage, muscle recovery time is reduced.

To use "the stick" on the calf muscle (most important in running), start each stroke at the Achilles tendon and roll up the leg toward the knee. Gently roll back to the origin and continue, repeatedly. For the first 5 minutes a gentle rolling motion will bring additional blood flow to the area. As you gradually increase the pressure on the calf during an "up" stroke, you'll usually find some "knots" or sore places in the muscles. Concentrate on these as you roll over them again and again, gradually breaking up the tightness.

Foam Roller—self massage for IT band, hip, etc.

This cylinder of dense foam is about 6 inches in diameter and about one foot long. We've not seen any mode of treatment for Iliotibial band injury that has been more effective. For best effect, put the roller on the floor, and lie on your side so that the irritated IT band area is on top of the roller. As your body weight presses down on the roller, roll up and down on the area of the leg you want to treat. Roll gently for 2-3 minutes and then apply more pressure as desired. This is actually a deep tissue massage that you can perform on yourself. For IT band, we recommend rolling it before and after running.

Accelerade—best for hydration

This sports drink has a patented formula shown to improve recovery. Drinking it before and after prolonged, dehydrating workouts also helps to improve hydration. We recommend having a half-gallon container of Accelerade in the refrigerator. Drink 4-8 oz every 1-2 hours, throughout the day. Best time to "top off" your fluid levels is within 24 hours before a long run. Prime time for replacing fluids is during the 24-hour period after a long run. Many runners have 32 oz or so in a thermos, for sipping during walk breaks in a prolonged speed training session. I suggest adding about 25% more water than recommended.

Research has also shown that drinking Accelerade about 30 min before running can get the body's startup fuel (glycogen) activated more effectively, and may conserve the limited supply of this crucial fuel.

Endurox R4—for recovery

This product has almost "cult following" status among runners. In fact, the research shows that the 4:1 ratio of carbohydrate to protein helps to reload the muscle glycogen more quickly (when consumed within 30 min of the finish of a hard or long workout. This means that the muscles feel bouncy and ready to do what you can do, sooner. There are other anti-oxidants in R4 that speed recovery.

Vitamins

I now believe that most runners need a good vitamin to boost the immune system and resist infection. There is some evidence that getting the proper vitamin mix can also speed recovery. The vitamin line I use is called Cooper Complete. Dr. Kenneth Cooper (founder of the Cooper Clinic and the Aerobics Institute), is behind this product. In the process of compiling the most formidable body of research on exercise and long-term health I've seen anywhere, he found that certain vitamins play important roles.